The Holy Year

The Holy Year

*Meditative Contemplations
of Seasons and Festivals*

FRIEDRICH RITTELMEYER

Floris
Books

Translated by Margaret Mitchell and Alan Stott
Edited by Neil Franklin

First published in German under the title *Das heilige Jahr*
by Verlag Urachhaus in 1930. Selections first published in English
in *The Christian Community Journal,* Vol. 1, Nos. 1–12
Reprinted in *The Christian Community Journal,*
Vol. 5, Nos. 9 & 10, Sept. – Oct. 1951. Published as *The Holy Year*
in 1951 by The Christian Community Press. This completed and
revised edition published in English by Floris Books in 2019

Unless otherwise indicated, Bible quotations are from
the New International Version

British Library CIP Data available
ISBN 978-178250-552-5
Printed in Great Britain
by TJ International

Contents

Foreword

The publication in English of this pioneering work about the Christian Year is made in time for the centenary of the Movement for Religious Renewal, The Christian Community in 2022. Amongst the founders, Friedrich Rittelmeyer was the first to occupy the leading position from its beginning until his death in 1938. After a period of much development, the reader today is in a better position to appreciate this classic work, *The Holy Year.*

We are not given a number of practical suggestions how to organise our celebrations. Instead, we are given descriptive sketches by a Christian priest and pastor that encourage people to become more perceptive of the time in which they are living. His attempts to deepen meditative insight are made precisely for the sake of stimulating creativity for organising meaningful religious celebrations.

Without attempts at renewal, it has to be acknowledged that in our age we are in danger of losing the great festivals of the spiritual or holy year. The call to re-enliven culture has become even more urgent and critical in the twenty-first century. The Christian mysticism offered here is inspiring and challenging at the same time – a sign of Rittelmeyer's achievement that he speaks so much that is relevant for our own time.

The author acknowledges the supporting natural seasons (in the temperate zone of the northern hemisphere) both of the time of preparation and withdrawal during the winter months, and of celebration as the earth breathes out in spring and summer. Spiritual struggle and spiritual ecstasy are encountered. In such a survey, to make no mention of our general and specific cultural heritage would be a marked loss – so we meet Shakespeare, Goethe, Paul, Raphael, Francis of Assisi, Meister Eckhart, Angelus Silesius, Dürer, Grünewald and others, including more than a nod to Nietzsche – but also the great religious founders and deep thinkers – Zarathustra, the Buddha, Mencius, Plato, Moses, Luther and Rudolf Steiner. The essence of these great original figures of human history, along with references to classical and Teutonic mythology, as well as fairytales, assist the author's endeavour – through imaginative and reasoned speculation, reflection, mysticism, anecdote, aphorism and simple homiletic narration – to inspire a new approach to enliven the course of the year.

Rittelmeyer's crafted sketches also contain abundant references to scripture, in particular John's Gospel from which he drew particular strength (sharing his meditative yield in other publications). He was, no doubt, a child of his age and culture. Building on the mystics, poets and thinkers that he quotes, Rittelmeyer also ventures to share his own meditative discoveries. Dante undertook the greatest inner journey, accompanied by the Roman poet Virgil – so why not attempt a mini-version in today's context with an angelic companion? Again, a particular period of forced rest during convalescence brought a rich meditative reward – why not share that episode with his people?

Detractors of Rittelmeyer suggest he may have been too ambitious here and there, too 'romantic' – is he not indulgent or controversial in his honesty? People point to his position as a 'transitional' personality – forgetful of the fact that every scholar and pastor lives a transitional role. True, some of the author's statements may appear incomplete in the light of improved religious sympathies that have developed since the time of writing. Other colleagues, in particular Hermann Beckh, provided more comprehensive viewpoints in careful, detailed work. It is nevertheless a fact that much fruitful research came from the younger colleagues who acknowledged Rittelmeyer's insights on John's Gospel, in particular Rudolf Frieling, Rudolf Meyer and later Christoph Rau.

An appreciation of Rittelmeyer in English was written by Adam Bittleston, 'Friedrich Rittelmeyer as Forerunner of a Christianity of the Future'.[1] All told, with his generous heart and will to serve, Rittelmeyer, a man of prayer, born preacher and pastor of souls, emerges as a pioneer of a new spiritual age. His work is distinctly relevant to the challenges facing us today.

These chapters originally appeared in the monthly journal *Die Christengemeinschaft*, which began in April 1924 (taking over from *Tatschristentum* that was issued during 1923). *Das Heilige Jahr* is a selection of the products of his pen from the first issue onwards. In 1932 twelve articles translated by Margaret Mitchell appeared in English in *The Christian Community Journal*, and were published as a pamphlet in 1951. We have revised and corrected Margaret Mitchell's translation of the selection, translated the missing sections, added references and some explanatory notes. My thanks to my wife for help making the translation, the late Margaret Miles who began editing, to Dr Neil Franklin for giving of his time and the riches of his wisdom in many helpful ways, and to Christian Maclean at Floris Books who made many helpful suggestions.

Alan Stott, Ascension 2018

Preface

This book goes out in a time of deep unrest trembling through humanity. The author, not unmoved but undisturbed by the daily alarms, seeks his place among those working for the future. If he succeeds in building a temple of quietness in stormy years from which triumphant, transfiguring forces flow for a number of people, then is his wish fulfilled.

Similar things, which at one time were contained in the old books of sermons and commentaries of our parents, still hold good for a completely changed humanity. The collected articles here – which for the most part appeared in the monthly journal *Die Christengemeinschaft* – are shorter than the old Bible contemplations and more universal. Above all, however, they are meditatively filled, born out of inner contemplation and intended for inner contemplation. In such a way they hope for find the hearts of contemporary people better, and to fulfil their needs better, than the 'books of edification' whose time is past.

The use this book will make is the reader's business. Yet a suggestion may be offered. For whoever reads these contemplations on Saturday evening and then recalls them on the morning of Sunday or festival day, to a certain extent wakes up in them, lets them live for a while in the early morning and work in one's being, then during the course of the day to allow them to resound within oneself, they will be most profitable.

The explanations are chiefly structured to allow themselves to be formed into a picture. In this way they can accompany us into the week, as picture and word with what enlivens our soul on Sunday. From week to week we can so walk through the year, and not just *one* year. If there is not a contemplation for each of the 52 weeks, then the reader has the possibility to look back, to draw together, and, if need be, to repeat the meditation.

Intensive meditation appears to me as the most important thing for modern people, if they are not to break down through the combined effects of outer pressures and an inner hollowing out. How one meditates and learns to meditate I have written about more fully in my book, *Meditation*. The pictures from the Gospel of John described there are not in contradiction to what is offered here, but supplementary.

But let it also be said that even a person far from Christianity can freely find fruits from the contents of this book. Perhaps the contemplations are also suited to be read aloud and discussed in small circles. Only be warned against one thing: do not read the book all at once as though for writing a press review. That would be like someone consuming all the provisions meant for a journey through the desert at one go beforehand – and then wondering why he has indigestion instead of being nourished.

So this book is a diary to last. It is essential for contemporary people to learn again to lift themselves above the daily concerns, to learn to celebrate festivals and into their hard life to weave real sun-days.

Advent

World stillness

When the season of Advent begins, one may recall the legend about the devil, for whom the Christmas festival was a thorn in the flesh. 'If I don't put down the Christmas festival, then every year mankind will get a longing for heaven again, and Christianity cannot be uprooted.' For a long time he brooded, becoming ever thinner and paler and more miserable. Then suddenly he cried, 'I have it!' What did he have? He had discovered Christmas fever. And since then people are overcome by a feverish rush in the time before Christmas. The trader must profit – now the number of shopping days to Christmas is announced – and when Christmas Eve arrives, the husband is worn out and shattered. Perhaps he can still count his money, but first of all he must have a really good sleep. But the housewife, who has to think of all the children and relations, of all the aunts and uncles, sinks down on the sofa exhausted on Christmas Eve. 'Leave me in peace! I can do no more!'

All the fine feelings that would come to the fore at Christmas time to connect mankind again with the infinite and to tell them of their forgotten heavenly origin are deadened by those two servants of the devil, Noise and Hurry. This is the work of God's enemies on the human soul.

For one who really experiences the season of Advent it is as if a thousand voices are audible on the earth. There is something that says within: you must become absolutely quiet if you want to hear what is around you and what is there for you. Veils are laid over nature's many colours. But these veils are like living spirits who now want to speak, as so often the drifting morning mist bears some promise of things to come.

No evening in Advent should pass without our listening to the stillness. Even when no single graspable thought comes, we feel we are quite close to the world's creation. It engulfs us as when 'the Spirit moved over the face of the deep'. The Father of the world holds back his world in the spirit, from which it originates, so that it may come forth from him again new-decked in heavenly glory.

He holds us back, too. We spend time again in the land of promise and presentiment. We rest once more in the very womb of spiritual growth and are enveloped in all the hopes for our future. We are fed with new courage and new hope from the fullness of God.

And then we look outside and it seems as if 'the lost Word' were once more bestowed on creation. The sun considers whether it should not rather re-sound then shine. The stars come very close to people, as if in the next moment they would speak, as if they cannot wait to tell their secret. Their beaming eyes now inspect the earth to see what has become of it, and they are amazed to see what has become of it, and they are amazed to see now lifeless mankind still is. The fields look dead, as though concealing treasure of which they may not tell. The woods and mountains become silent under the heavens, awaiting the word of 'those on high'. Even the water in the river becomes pensive, it communes and contemplates Becoming.

Everything becomes prophetic; all the prophets silently point to that which is to come.

The sun says, 'See how my light is extinguished! I am not your sun!'

The stars proclaim, 'The heavenly worlds live over you that you do not yet know! Look out for him who brings you the key to open them!'

The dying world speaks with a thousand voices, 'We all return to our spiritual home. Where is your road to heaven? Have you not heard of him who is 'the Way' to the heights, and 'the Truth' that abides in the starry sky above you, and 'the Life' that the earthly sun cannot give?'

But our own soul begins to murmur, too. 'Do you really know me? Do you know that I have already collected treasures that you carry in yourself without knowing it? Do you know that you can find in my depths wells in which the stars are reflected? That the depths and the heights are one? Do you know that I could tell you many wonders that you have forgotten? Do you know that you are the lord of a castle who thinks only about that castle, but in the rocks under him there is a world where treasure chests await the fortunate one, where precious stones sparkle like eyes that can look up to the stars?'

Advent is a solemn season. Holiness descends and once more envelops us. If we enter into its creative movement and purpose, then for a time it allows us to behold our own divine image. The Advent dream which we have once again dreamed in the divine womb of all creation seeks to wake into 'new year'.

The soul itself now wants to become receptive for the Star from above, for the holy 'I-am', for the divine Son. It desires peace and quiet to become 'mother'. The mystery of mother and child hovers over it. It wants to become this mystery itself. Then will the shining Son be born therein.

Promise

When the sun is about to rise the mountain peaks begin to glow. They turn towards the approaching light and then tell of it to people in the valley. So centuries before the coming of Christ great men towered up like mountain peaks and spoke to those below about him 'Who shall come'. People called them prophets. We think of them during Advent, before the sun rises on Christmas Day.

The peaks light up not only in the Holy Land. Also in China, in India, in Greece the red of dawn glowed – before once again the fog of the last centuries came and the last cold shiver passed over the earth.

In China four centuries before Christ, next to the two great leaders Lao Tse and Confucius, there appeared a third, though lesser known, whose teaching is more significant, Mencius (Mengzi).

If there is no reciprocal love in the state, the strong will lay hold of the weak, the rich sneer at the poor, the distinguished despise the lowly, the cunning cheat the dullards. All misery, arrogance, discontent in the land originate from lack of love of one for another ... This is the meaning of love: love what the other has as your own! And, love the other as yourself ... the effectiveness of heaven lies in our being absolutely without self-seeking. Its gift is wealth without restriction, its light lasting without exception. That is why the holy ones took it as their ideal. If heaven is law, then we must think about heaven in our work; we should do what heaven wishes, leave undone what heaven does not wish. What does heaven wish for, what does it hate?

It wishes that people love one another, that they help one another, and does not wish that they hate each other and rob each other. How does one know this? Because it loves without exception, it helps everyone without exception. It owns all and nourishes all.[1]

Mencius divines in the outer heaven the inner heaven. That was his great prophetic insight. But the proclamation of love first gained its world-conquering power when this heaven itself came down and as a visible human being walked amongst men. Christ could point to himself and say that the heavenly Father 'causes his sun rise on the evil and the good' (Mt 5:45).

There is a noble song of love in India, too. From the mouth of the holy Buddha came the words:

> All the means in this life of gaining religious merit,
> O monks, do not have one sixteenth the value
> of love, the heart's redemption. Love, the heart's
> redemption, surpasses them and shines, burns and
> radiates. And, O monks, as the light of all the stars
> has not a sixteenth the value of moonlight, but
> the moonlight surpasses it and shines, burns and
> radiates, so too, O monks, have all the means in
> this life of gaining religious merit not one sixteenth
> the value of love, the heart's redemption. Love,
> the heart's redemption, surpasses them and shines,
> burns and radiates. And as, O monks, in the last
> month of the rainy season, in autumn, the sun in
> the clear, cloud-free sky rising into the heavens,
> removed from everything dark in the airy spaces,
> shines, burns and radiates, and as in the night, in
> the early morning, the Morning Star shines, burns
> and radiates, so, O monks, have all the means in

this life of gaining religious merit not one sixteenth the value of love, the heart's redemption. Love, the heart's redemption surpasses them and shines, burns and radiates.[2]

With these words Gautama Buddha seems like a brother of the Apostle Paul, who sang the great Song of Love (1Cor 13). But did Buddha bring love or had he only a presentiment of it? The holy man of India stands before us with his proclamation as if the grace of a future world flowed round him, like a Moses on Mount Nebo.

At that time also the mountain peak of Greece began to glow.

Mark well, O Socrates! He who has been educated thus far in love – after he has been gradually led from outer beauty to inner beauty – will finally, at the last consecration of his love, see a wondrous sight and behold the great beauty of creation ... He will gaze upon beauty that is for itself and in itself beautiful, that mirrors itself eternally; and whatever else is beautiful will only appear so, and be only a part. And there, my dear Socrates, cried the prophetess, there if anywhere at all, is life worth living, where you behold eternal beauty ... Do you believe your life or that of anyone else would still be base when you might gaze thereon and remain in the presence of that wonder?[3]

Just another step, one imagines, and love of beauty must become the beauty of love.

To the same Greek culture that Plato spoke, Paul a few centuries later wrote 'Now we see only a reflection as in a mirror; then we shall see face to face. Now I know in part; then I shall know fully, even as I am fully known' (1Cor 13:12).

In the Holy Land yet deeper things were seen than in the great lands of the spirit, China, India and Greece. Isaiah remains the greatest of the prophets.

> Surely he took up our pain and bore our suffering,
> yet we considered him punished by God, stricken
> by him, and afflicted. But he was pierced for our
> transgressions, he was crushed for our iniquities: the
> punishment that brought us peace was on him, and
> by his wounds we are healed ... Therefore I will give
> him a portion among the great, and he will divide
> the spoils with the strong, because he poured out his
> life unto death (Is 53:4f, 12).

The Chinese looked from the life values to the universal blessing of love.

The Indians saw from the religious striving to the ultimate consecrating power of love.

The Greeks gazed forth from the longing of love towards the heavenly beauty of love.

It is like a prophecy of thinking, feeling and will. But from trouble and affection the Israelite looked prophetically towards the divine-human reality of love in Christ. He looked towards the 'I' that loves.

Expectation

In the time before Christmas Christians of all centuries have concentrated on John the Baptist. With John the Baptist they have waited for Christ and longed for Christ. John the Baptist is the epitome of humanity's expectation and longing. In his greatness is everything that anticipated Christ. The expectation is not just an individual wish but the yearning of humanity itself for Christ. That is why it is good to study him before we come to Christ.

'Are you the one who is to come, or should we expect someone else?' This is the question that John poses in the story (Mt 11:3; Lk 7:19). And thus do we stand in him before Christ. He had experienced great things concerning Christ, indeed the greatest. But there is much he cannot grasp. He had hoped for a great sweep forwards – but everything goes so terribly slowly. He wanted to see fulfilment – but instead of the full-blazing sun, only the dawn. The divine should manifest itself fully – but everything remains hidden.

Who does not know those stumbling blocks by which people are constantly entangled in relation to Christ? It is the antithesis of earth and heaven. Heaven wants to come to earth, but the earth expects earth.

Moreover, the great opposition in the world to Christ that is now prepared is, from our viewpoint, the hatred of disillusionment. Christianity has not done enough for the overcoming of evil, for the victory of righteousness. So little is done against the prevailing powers that it appears to be in league with them.

In many struggles over Christianity we can see the disappointed John. And we see deepest when we see him.

A prophet also lives deep within us. Man's seeing heart is the original prophet whence all others have arisen. Since Paradise he has lived in everyone. Time after time he pronounces what man should be according to his divine destiny, now with great passion, now with a quiet lamenting – like the prophets of Israel. We want to listen into this original prophet when he sends his message to Christ in the days before Christmas: 'Are you he who is to come or shall we look for another?' That one shall come we all basically know. But is it Christ?

As surely as man has intelligence, as surely he has a right to question and an obligation to verify. The greatest of men, as

Christ called the Baptist, himself questioned. Following his lead, all of us put the decisive question to Christ; like John, we put the question while 'in prison' – for Plato was right: the human soul is in the prison of earthly existence.

And with John we want to listen to Christ as if we were the listening soul of the whole of humanity: 'Go back and report to John what you have seen and heard: The blind receive sight, the lame walk, those who have leprosy are cleansed, the deaf hear, the dead are raised, and the good news is proclaimed to the poor' (Lk 7:22).

Where today is the fulfilment about which Christ spoke? Today Christ answers from our inner being, just as from our inner being John asked.

What would life be like for us without the light that shines from Christ? Have we not learnt to see our neighbours quite differently? And the future of humanity? And heaven? *The blind receive their sight.*

And do we not know that when we only think on Christ, we take surer steps? That we feel raised up when his name resounds in us? That we slowly come nearer to higher goals, find clear paths, sense growing powers to move forwards? *The lame walk.*

And when we think on the sickness of sin, do we not feel how a healing from within has begun? How we now first know what real purity *is,* even if its part in us is so small? *Those who have leprosy are cleansed.*

Do not long since forgotten voices sound in our soul as if news came to us that we have always awaited and for which in daily life we had become unreceptive? *The deaf hear.*

And do we not begin to divine what life is? Are there not times when we feel the victory over all death like music in our souls? When a buried eternity arises? *The dead are raised.*

Are not we ourselves the poor – if we consider the depths of our souls? Have we not already renounced the idea that the promise should be fulfilled in our souls? Was it not that which really made us poor? Do we not experience what rich worlds would open to us even if the fulfilment is different from the promise? *The good news is proclaimed to the poor.*

It is *in us* that the whole story really takes place – both the question of the prophet and the answer of the mighty One approaching. That we let the story take place in us is a preparation for Christmas. Nothing could better prepare us for Christmas.

In the outer world, too, we see the first signs of fulfilment, however small today they may be.

We also get other eyes for the becoming of our Christian Community.

Let us not wait for the completed task, but work in the first stages.

The only proof of Christ are his deeds. So let us constantly in the present, too, take the message of Christ's deeds to a questioning humanity – Christ's deeds for us, and then Christ's deeds through us. Speaking deeds are the transformed gospel of Christmas Eve.

Christmas

Christmas Eve

The struggle for the continued celebration of Christmas Eve is a struggle that concerns our whole culture. If Christmas is lost through hurry and exhaustion, swallowed up in external and meaningless concerns, then the very core of our culture is gone.

It is a struggle for the child. If when we are children, Christmas is for us a blessed and happy time, then it leaves behind a golden radiance in our lives, whatever else happens to us. Anyone who does not carry Christmas joy in their heart has not been a child in the full sense of the word.

It is a struggle for spiritual power. If we lose the festival of Christmas, then the last fountain of divine strength in people's souls will be dried up. We are very near to losing it. You have only to read the Christmas articles in the newspapers, even those written by representatives of the churches: a weary war against the forces of destruction and decay; feeble thoughts about the usefulness of Christmas; painful endeavours to show that it 'still' has meaning. No triumphal steps forward; no new age.

Widukind, the Germanic leader of the Saxon, crept into the camp of his mighty opponent, Charlemagne. He longed to know what it was that gave Christians their power.

At midnight on Christmas Eve he witnessed the Holy Mass. A little shining child – so it seemed to him – appeared in the host that was raised at the altar. He bowed his savage heart before the golden brilliance of the Child, who seemed to beckon to him.

The rude chieftain beheld with the eyes of his childlike soul what the Emperor of the Franks, himself a messenger of Christ, did not see. Once again arose man's age-old power of beholding the Highest when it draws near.[1]

The festival of Christmas became the favourite festival of the Germanic peoples. But the vision faded. Now is the time for its return. Beholding in the event at the altar the being of Christ will mean the beginning of a new Christmas festival.

Is there such a being as a Christmas angel? Yes, an angel of the festival of Christmas is indeed at work in the world. Not Christ himself, but one of his intimate servants. To him Christmas is entrusted. We can speak with him and allow him to tell us how Christmas should be celebrated. This invisible leader of the Christmas feast will open for us new kingdoms of the soul.

World Ash Tree – Christmas Tree. The World-Tree or Yggdrasil of Norse mythology has come into our homes, just as the life of humanity has become something carefully tended and civilised – in comparison with its cosmic dimensions in earlier times. When we see in the Christmas tree the new World Ash Tree, then Central Europe's age of the Spirit will have begun. In its crown it is not an eagle that builds its eyrie, but a star that shines. Its branches are not gnawed by the powers of destruction, but upon them burn the lights of life. At its feet no deadly dragon makes its lair, but there lies the harvest field of love. Two worlds! For Christ has changed the world!

Our gaze rises to the starry heavens. There shines the true World-Tree. The stars are the thousand lights kindled by the Almighty himself. The earth is the table of presents below. But only the soul can see the star on top: 'I AM!'

> And from his darkest night
> The Lord he steps afar,
> And ties once more the threads
> Which had been torn apart.[2]

Is not the Christmas Tree also a picture of the threefold Christian star of light, love and life? It radiates the divine splendour of *light*. It proclaims the *life* that outlasts earthly winter. It gives an inkling of the depths of *love*. Where Christmas is truly kept, we find strivings of love both human and divine. Human love is permeated with divine love. Divine love flows into human love.

Children have a right to expect from us a holy Christmas Eve. What an untruth the Christmas Tree is if it does not shine in our own hearts! How cold the gifts if we do not give *ourselves* with them! How false and dead the Christmas carols if we do not sing them with our soul! On this Eve our children are right to expect us to be with them in the world of childhood and then to go with us into the world of the divine Child. There is nothing more lovely told of Schiller than how on Christmas Eve he sat under the Christmas Tree and gazed into the light.

Only children can celebrate Christmas. It is the feast of the divine Child. If we would enter the holy temple of Christmas, neither gifts nor money will help us, only the desire to become young.

What is it that children can do better than grown-ups? There are three arts at which they are geniuses. They can *listen*.

Look at children when they are told a fairy story. They take it in with their whole being. This is the first act of Christmas.

Children can *be happy*. There is no more lovely picture in the world than that of a happy child in whose pure, untroubled eyes the Christmas Tree is reflected. To be able to be happy is the second art of Christmas.

Children can *trust*. Even on the window sill they sleep peacefully if their mother has laid them here. To entrust oneself to the power of the divine life that shines into our existence is the ultimate art of Christmas.

If we would celebrate Christmas in a Christian way, we must have within us a shepherd and a king: a shepherd who can listen to what others do not hear; who with all his strength of devotion lives directly under the starry heaven; to whom the angel can long to reveal it. And a king who can offer gifts; who takes his guidance from nothing but the star on high; who gets out to bring all his gifts to a crib.

And as well as a shepherd and a king there must also be in us a child who now waits to be born.

The clock strikes twelve. The bells burst into sound. A sea of sound flows harmoniously through the dark air. The earth begins to sing. Metal from the depths of the earth has come into the upper world. It has been formed into a cup and as it swings it tries to turn heavenward to be filled. Age-long subterranean silence rises up to speak in the ringing of the bells, full of inspiration, yet without words. And just as imagination and inspiration are there, so too is intuition: in the undulations of the sound of the bells life streams into all the corners of our soul and forcefully tells us what no words can say.

If we really experience night in its contrast to day, we must be able to experience its light, its music and its nourishment.

We do not know what night essentially is if we have not looked into its very heart.

In the angels' song of praise night awakens.

'Glory to God in the heights': the night becomes radiant.

'Peace on earth': the night resounds.

'To men of goodwill': the night becomes a source of nourishment.

In the holy night of Christmas, night itself is baptised at the fount of all creation. The Holy Spirit draws near and dips it in the light of revelation. The divine Son draws near and fills it with heavenly peace. God the Father himself draws near and fills it with his divine will.

If the night is baptised at the winter solstice, then all our coming day will be – Christmas.

Go out under the stars and experience the mighty act of consecration of the universe. There the divine Word speaks from heaven with a thousand voices. There is Gospel. There is Sermon. There is Creed.

And now the far spaces make Offering. The earth glows with devotion. It rises up to heaven like a cup, and round the cup flow prayers of offering.

Human beings themselves experience Transformation as never before. They become different. It is as if everything were permeated with higher being.

The great Communion between heaven and earth comes to fulfilment in the human being. The human being himself is this communion.

Two Christmas carols might sing in every heart. First comes the medieval song about Mary, *Es ist ein Ros' entsprungen:*

There is a flower springing
From tender roots it grows
From Eden beauty bringing.
From Jesse's stem as rose.
On his green branch it blows:
A bud that in cold winter
At midnight will unclose.

The deep feeling and faith of the Catholic Middle Ages lives right into the present in this carol. It is sung as from a thousand submerged churches in our midst.

Next to it rays the lights of the Reformation in Luther's carol:

The eternal light descends below
And makes the world anew to glow
It lights indeed the deep midnight
And makes us children of the light.

These verses span human history. The world's great drama is set before us in typical childlike yet powerful words.

Where the spirit of the one and the feeling of the other are in harmony, there you have the great Christian festival.

When the warm heartedness of Luke's Gospel and the great spirituality of John's Gospel are united, then is Christmas complete.

'I am – the light of the world.' Therewith all peoples are united. In the Jews and the Greeks we see their main representatives. The Jews worshipped the 'I AM'. It was their name for God. The Greeks looked up with awe and reverence to the 'light'. Apollo was their most beloved god. Zeus also takes his name from the 'shining heavens'.

In Christ the temple of Zeus and the temple of Yahweh become one. 'I am – the light of the world.'

Again Greeks and Jews – and with them all peoples – come together in the other Christmas pronouncement: 'The Word – became flesh.'

The Jews sought the word, listened to the word. Their prophets were living divine word; so, too, their tablets of the law.

The Greeks revered the body as the temple of the divine. They prayed with their eyes. In beauty they beheld the god with joyful devotion.

The Word – became flesh. The body – became Word. Christ appeared as the fulfilment of human longing.

The song of the Holy Night became day. When the Christ-child grew up, the pronouncement rang out: 'I am the light of the world. Whoever follows me will never walk in darkness, but will have the light of life' (Jn 8:12).

Do we hear again the song of Christmas Eve?

Then it said, 'Glory to God in the heights'; now there is heard, 'I am the light of the world'. The 'Peace on earth'; now is 'Whoever follows me shall not walk in darkness'. Then, 'to men of goodwill'; now, 'but shall have the light of life.'

Christmas Eve has become Day. It has become Human. It has become Life. And in us, too, the Holy Night would become Day, Human and Life!

Twelve Holy Nights[3]

Christmas Eve had come to humanity. The brass band played from the nearby church tower the chorale *'Vom Himmel hoch da komm' ich her'* (From highest heaven come I here).[4] It sounded as if men's soul had been fused into the notes, which sang the joyous news from the highest heaven down into earthly existence. On his bed lay a helpless man. He had overtaxed himself in his zeal for work and had to pay for it with disablement. With faces lit by joy, people passed through the house and were hurrying with their presents. To him, too, they intended to bring joy. Might they bring in his tree? Sing him a Christmas carol? But for him the joy was too much. Everything hurt him. Slowly the curtain of life closed around him. But while absolute silence surrounded him, and the people brought him only the daily food, a world of wonder was gloriously revealed in him. It was always in the night, as though angels came and put a picture before his soul that then remained in silent splendour the whole night through. It was absorbed into the sleep of the next night, and was replaced by a new picture.

He was a child. There lay a purity in his eyes as if one looked into divine worlds. Around the *Child* was an indescribable goodness, like radiant light. One only had to gaze upon the lovely, wonderful countenance, as if there were unending secrets to drink in. As if the Child had strayed into the human world from Paradise, where it had played from eternity under the eyes of the Father-God, as if too on earth he could never say anything but, 'I had to be in my Father's house'? (Lk 2:49).

When the sick man looked into the joyous light of this Child's eyes, it was as though everything in him became young again, indeed, for the first time young, as if everything in him dipped into the well of youth of all the worlds of heaven.

The image sank away and its disappearance left a yearning homesickness in his heart. But another image sought the soul. There by the lake a silent expectant crowd of people. Softly murmuring waves come as if from far away towards the shore. Peacefully the white clouds steer through the sky. In paradisal happiness the butterflies sway on the light-filled breezes. But there is a boat, upon which all eyes were fastened – was that really human language? Can human speech sound like that? It was spirit and life, holy spirit, as it had never lived in a man, life surging with light that like a breath from the furthest heights touched their dreaming souls. So it spoke to them of the kingdom of heaven that is *here*. The divine *Teacher of all peoples* and times stood before the people and they did not know it, hardly divined it. All the heavens listened.

On this evening the silent man felt as if everything surged around him from unimagined depths.

As he awoke the next morning, it appeared that endless events had taken place in the meantime. Beseeching eyes from all sides. Longing hands raised from many sick-beds. The need of the world had opened up as if it had heard the call that it had always awaited. With inexpressible goodness one figure bent over a sick man. As he put his hand on him, it appeared heavy with blessing and light with living spirit right into each vein. Healing flowed in dreams from this One through hand, mouth and eye. Nature round about breathed out a sigh. They all came to take and draw for their sick life. The great *World Physician* went through his kingdom.

The longer indeed the sufferer gazed on this image the more it was for him as if a healing hand was laid on his head, too.

It was good that the sick man was refreshed in this picture, for the next day brought difficulties. Before him stood a menacing, noble, upright figure. On his forehead flamed majesty as though the Ten Commandments from Sinai flashed there, or the mystery of which they were only an inkling. In his eyes blazed fire, as if the holy sacrificial ardour from Mount Carmel were there again, to consume for ever every opponent of God.[5] From his hand raised on high raged the Last Judgment. 'My house will be called a house of prayer, but you are making it a den of robbers' (Mt 21:13).

The solemnity shook the sick man right into his limbs, the solemnity of this apparition piercing through the world carrying final decision. He knew: I have beheld the *Judge*. And then there was no anxiety of spirit for him. He knew nothing other than complete surrender in devotion. It could not be otherwise. It could – it must be so!

An incredible holiness rises up out of the depths of the world. Singing as of unheard choirs of angels surrounded the resting man. He tried for a long time to listen. But it was as if he would need other senses to catch even the slightest sound. Only an inkling of unspeakable consecration of life reached him. Then he saw into the picture.

In the dim shining darkness of the world over which the starry depths flickered stood a man on a mountain. He stood still, who knows for how long already? Then he looked up and it was as if his eyes were akin to the brightest stars. Now one could also read – through the eyes – into his soul. 'Hallowed be thy name.' The whole strong soul had changed into prayer and glowed in purest might up to the stars: I have seen *God's Holy One*.

These words as heavenly sounds went through the heart of the one lying there on this day.

As morning approached, out of this picture a new picture appeared.

A man stood in a meadow. Around him, his friends. He had picked a wild flower, one of the thousands that grew there in the meadow. Now he looked into the flower-chalice as if he could see in that chalice the whole world as in a mirror. And the delicate petals opened and became precious garments. And the fine-smelling stamen became a king's sceptre. And in the depths of the cup a king's crown lit up. 'Yet I tell you that not even Solomon in all his splendour was dressed like one of these' (Mt 6:29; Lk 12:27). 'You of little faith' What is all your knowledge, when you cannot read the secret, no, the revealed writing of the Father of the world? Do you see there the *Wisest of the wise* is standing, from whose spirit light flows, pure shining light in all realms of existence?

The sick man did not have long to enjoy this picture. Lively movement went through his dreams the next night.

A hilly landscape. Over there a small group of people are moving around. The first person walks on as if a world was to be conquered. Those following him find it hard to keep up. His walk is like a defiance of all powers. His eye had looked upon all danger. On his forehead is written the challenge for the decisive battle for the world. His voice thunders as if from the most difficult victory. 'We are going up to Jerusalem' (Mk 10:33). And the widths of the world become transparent. In every land companies of heroes appear. All the heroes stop and look towards the *Hero of heroes*. They lower their swords in greeting towards him. Jerusalem rests still unknowing in all its cleverness, strength and evil. Soon it will have to fight with this One for life and death for all its honour.

During the night a winter thunderstorm passed over the land. As it became light again, the storm remained in the sick-room.

It was as if the lightning flashed from the eyes of a man, the black clouds were his angry thoughts and the rumbling thunder was his mighty voice – as the man stood on the Mount of Olives and looked over to the Temple. War and war cries. Eclipse of the sun and stars falling to the earth. Earthquakes and cries of lamentation. Fear and threats of persecution. Awake! Awake! Awake! The *Prophet* appeared out of the gentle Master and his gaze penetrates over space and time. Does he announce only world-pain? Speech breaks forth out of his prophetic mouth and remains towering above the end of the world: 'Heaven and earth will pass away, but my words will never pass away' (Mt 24:35, Mk 13:31, Lk 21:33).

Never had our lonely friend really known what a *Priest* is. During the following night, he experienced it.

Before him he saw a simple room in Jerusalem. A small circle of devoted, silent disciples saw him again. He raised the bread. In this way can the gifts of the earth be handled? Was it with one touch that the whole earth was also consecrated, changed? The earth lifted itself like a Grail dish that wants to receive the divine light. The raised look of thanks penetrated through all the clouds like a light that flashed over the whole sky. The Soul of All Love, however, saw the bread, blessed it and gave itself without measure.

When the disabled man took his bread that day he did not know what happened to him. As if he felt his way into mysteries which he could not explain. As if the high-priestly blessing streamed to him, the depth of which was hidden from him.

Yet the most solemn experiences were still to come for the one cut off from the world.

Turmoil of the crowds. Before the Governor stands a heavily bound man. Freezing scorn had pressed a crown on his forehead from which blood trickles down. Alone, without a helping hand from the whole round world, powerlessness that could not be greater, he stood facing the Roman worldly power. Silent, motionless, he allows himself to be pushed down into disgrace, pain and destruction. Nothing at all of earthly glory is to be seen on him. As if he himself accepted the judgement as right, he goes silently down into night. And yet what is this? Does he not carry his fetters as a king his sceptre? Does he not hold his peace as the world judgement itself? Majesty without comparison weaves its cloak around his wounded shoulders.

Heaven-born dignity radiates from his beaten body into the night of the soul around him. And now the walls of existence crack apart. The Roman Empire disappears as though by a magic wand. A new kingdom stands there! Gratitude, honour, devotion, jubilant praise streams towards the One from all peoples, from all parts of the world: 'Hail to Thee, O *King!*'

The sick man awoke next morning with a feeling of unspeakable pain. It was for him as if he had had tormenting dreams for aeons, as if he had wandered for millennia through hell.

The cross still stood, leaden. Hour upon hour pressed with the weight of the world upon the soul of the martyr. No longer came word came from his lips, as if he himself feared he would break with the movement. In his eyes such deep despair that a world could have died from it. Only a last flame deep in the background struggled with the light. People gossiped and laughed on the hill. But a breathless shiver went through all the heavenly spaces as if the angels could stir themselves no longer, as if death staring upwards from the earth had poisoned all radiant life in all the worlds of light.

The sufferer could not move all day, could only speak one word, only think one thought. The eyes of those caring for him betrayed to him, the end is soon approaching. And yet this day all his sufferings were healed for all time through the *Greatest of all Martyrs.*

As though sinking into an abyss, ever deeper and ever darker, the sick man at last fell asleep. He woke up to gentle super-earthly sounds.

Singing appeared to come from the depths of everything. As though songs were awakened which since the beginning were asleep in everything and had to await, bewitched into silence until this day. Absolutely everywhere became alive, as in preparation for the festival of festivals. The air itself appeared to live and beheld him with meaningful eyes. Never had he credited the ancient earth with such a fiery splendour! As if adorning itself to become Paradise again that it should be what the Creator once willed unending aeons ago. But who would have known that this Paradise is something so spiritually glorious, alive with light, breathing beauty that surpasses all divining? Divinity wide and near spread around him. In the middle, however, was a figure – indeed, as if all the stars and suns and a thousand suns and stars that he had not seen had borrowed their light from it. Was he light? Was he spirit? It was a single raying of purity and unfathomable goodness. Thus he spoke, thus he rayed forth: 'I AM,' so true, so mighty that one now felt for the first time what might and what reality is. And all creatures in all kingdoms, and all the angels in all the worlds sang a single song in a thousand choirs to the *Lord of Glory*.

Our friend did not know how long his soul had rested in this picture. Slowly it faded, as though carried away by angels into the heights. Then the bells began to chime. The people were celebrating Epiphany, the festival of the appearance of Christ. The man on his sick-bed smiled. The children told him that the Christmas tree had disappeared, that the Christmas room had changed back again to the daily living room. He listened, as if this whole world was a dream. Now life could bring what it will. He had received the consecration of all humanity.

Epiphany

The Three Wise Men

Visits full of secrecy from 'initiates', from people enlightened with divinity, full of wisdom, were not unusual in olden times. One thinks of what is told from the life of Tauler or of Jakob Boehme. The flat, sure 'No' that science today has for such stories can only raise a smile when one explores and experiences more deeply.

The possibility also exists that here, perhaps on the basis of real occurrences, a visionary experience is told, a meaningful inner picture spiritually true in which the cosmic meaning of the newborn child was experienced. The initiates, called 'kings' in the mystery language, did not need to carry crowns for the external world. The Wise Men from the East with their three symbolic gifts, however, represent the three most important cultures that flourished before the time of Christ. Gold signifies wisdom, which was sought above all in the ancient Persian culture seeking to see through the great opposites of existence and who called their divinely inspired leader Zarathustra, 'Star of Gold'. Incense represents the devotion-filled feeling, as it lived in the lofty development of the Indian culture, for us today hardly imaginable, and as it can still meet us today among eminent Indians. Myrrh, however, was highly held in the ancient world because of its healing forces, and thus it represents the Egyptian culture in which above all a training of the human will in the mystery centres was sought in the art of medicine. When the purest thinking, the most inward feeling, the strongest will is brought to Christ, then what the 'Adoration of the Magi' prophetically announced will be achieved. And wherever one of these three gifts that humanity alone can give is brought to Christ, one of the three kings is present – more than the place where their bodies are revered with terrible superstition.[1]

When in the Act of Consecration of Man the prayer is spoken that our pure thinking, our loving heart and our willing devotion would bring the offering, there this distant time is prepared; there the Three Kings are always bringing their gifts. We think back to the Christmas night. 'Glory to God in the heights, and peace on earth to men of good will.' Thus it has sounded in our soul during the days of Christmas. And now the Wise Men come from the East bringing gold, frankincense and myrrh. That is a sounding together of heaven and earth that has never been greater.

Heaven opens and radiates down its highest. And the earth opens up and brings its best. The sounding together is accomplished in the human being.

The revelation 'glory to God in the highest' wants to enter human beings and where it is received, thinking is changed into purest gold. The 'glory of the Lord' lights up within.

And 'peace on earth' rays back the beams of heaven, and all the feeling in human hearts changes into devotion, into sacrificial reverence, what incense throughout the millennia seeks to express.

The 'good will', however, awakens and healing forces stream from all the will of humanity as the myrrh presages and displays.

Heaven and earth meet in the human being. The heights of heaven call and the depths of the earth answer. Mankind is the dialogue between heaven and earth. One cannot express it more sublimely than as the sounding together of these two stories.

What is included there, is told in majestic images in the story of the greatest German poet, in Goethe's *Fairy Tale of the Green Snake and the Beautiful Lily*.

In a Temple a young man awakens to new life: Three kings speak to him.

The Golden King admonishes him, 'Know the highest.'

The Silver King speaks, 'Feed the sheep.'

The Brazen King adds to this: 'The sword in the left hand, the right hand free!'

Do we not also want to awaken on the earth as in the temple? Goethe calls to us not only, 'Know yourself,' as once in the Greek temple, but 'Know the highest.' Is it not pitiful how we always think in circles here on the earth? We have no idea what we could know of divine secrets in one single day, were we not distracted from continually beholding 'the highest'.

How much would a higher spirit behold were he in *our* position but went through life with *his* eyes! 'This is eternal life, that they know you, the only true God, and Jesus Christ, whom you have sent,' says Christ in the Great Petition, the High Priestly Prayer (Jn 17:3). Every day would bring eternal life in its fullness had we followed the admonitions of the Golden King, 'Know the highest!'

And the Silver King opens his mouth, 'Feed the sheep!' We know these words come from the end of John's Gospel. Once I asked an important man how one would know for certain if it really were Christ that one felt in the soul. The answer I received left a deep impression. Christ is the purest selflessness. On this alone one recognises him. 'By this everyone will know that you are my disciples, if you love one another' (Jn 13:35). What does one see, what do those around us see of 'pure selflessness' in our deeds? 'Feed the sheep!'

Also we could illuminate this saying from the Temple with a saying of Christ himself from the High-Priestly Prayer: 'They are yours; you gave them to me and they have obeyed your word' (Jn 17:6).

Now the third king, the king of will, joins in. 'The sword in the left hand, the right hand free.' Brave and free for each deed that we are called to do! Nobody should relinquish the faith that God plans a great deed through them, Luther said. If there were ever a time that had no use for battle-shy people, it is our own. Above all we must battle for Christ. He does not need dreamers today but heroes. We should be prepared right into each new conversation that we have, to fight for him, often just when we least expected it. But still the sword in the scabbard and the right hand free for creative work! And again we can illuminate the saying of the temple king with a saying of Christ from the High-Priestly Prayer: 'I have brought you glory on earth by finishing the work you gave me to do' (Jn 17:4).

We receive consecration for all our external life: strong and free!

A consecration for our life with people: selflessly giving,
and a consecration of our inner life: awake,
beholding God.

He who receives this consecration awakens in the Temple. In him everything is transformed into gold, frankincense and myrrh, in as much as he has fully taken in the heavenly hymn:

Glory to God in the heights,
and on the earth peace to men of good will.

The baptism of Christ

The Child over whom the angels sang, became a man. We see him by the Jordan at the time of the Baptism. The heavens open above him. Like a dove the Holy Spirit descends on him. A voice declares: 'You are my Son, whom I love; with you I am well pleased' (Mk 1:11, Lk 3:22).

A greater event has never been experienced. A shining temple in the farthest heights surrounded man for the first time.

Now *day* broke over the earth. Do we recognise again the night that has changed into day?

And as the world of the angels sounded, 'Glory to God in the heights,' here, too, the heavens open. Holy shrines of all life and being are opened. The world depths greet the Chosen One.

As then 'Peace on earth' was proclaimed – so here the heart of the universe lets its voice sound and speak of him as the beloved Son, upon whom God's revelation lovingly rests. So heaven itself points to the One in whom it can get a foothold amongst humanity. Thus here the earth itself becomes a stage to which passing spirits from distant worlds look down.

And as then the saying about 'men of good will' resounded – so here white shining life descends and the Holy Spirit begins its history on the earth. 'I will ... put a new spirit in you' (Ezk 36:26).

That was the Baptism in which Jesus became Christ. What needs to be seen is not what John the Baptist did by the Jordan. The *Father* from the highest realms looks down: 'Glory to God in the heights.' The heavens are opened. The *Son* is born, however, in the words of the Father, 'This is my beloved Son.' Peace on earth with heaven. And the *Holy Spirit* appears amongst men. The white dove draws in. The 'good will' is there. Thus in deeds the 'name' of the Father,

41

of the Son and of the Holy Spirit is spoken. That is the archetype of all baptisms.

What happened here then develops into the 'Gospel'. The *first* words with which Christ in John's Gospel speaks to his own, 'You will see the heavens open.'

The *most inward* word, the soul of his proclamation, 'I and the Father are one ... the Father is in me, and I in the Father' (Jn 10:30, 38). Peace.

The *final* word: 'It is finished,' – I have accomplished the work which you have given me to do (Jn 19:30). That was in truth the 'good will'.

Thus the angels' song of praise becomes a human soul. Thus the message of the angels becomes a human life.

A thousand songs still slumber in the Gospel, which no one has heard. One of the most splendid is how the Holy Night, Christmas Eve, changes to the Holy Day. The day of the earth rises from the night of Bethlehem.

All our days can now take their light from this day, as *all* our nights from Christmas Eve. What a day that would become!

Our day is filled with thinking, feeling and doing. Thinking receives the consecration of Christ when it seeks the open heaven on all sides. In ancient India people still knew of this secret. The spirit speaks to man in every earthly thing: 'Through this window I come into you' – thus proclaim the Vedas. And the noblest longing of the contemporary person also knows of it. 'To stand over everything as its own heaven,' that is Nietzsche's longing.[2] Through Christ comes the fulfilment. Above ourselves and our destiny, our eyes illumined by him always divine the open heavens. Our question reaches out above the person we meet, to his heaven, which our eyes always seek to find. Over every event, over every thing, over every duty a secret heaven arches which our eyes always seek to find.

And our feeling receives the consecration of Christ when we become a 'son', a child of God. 'This is my beloved Son in whom I am well pleased' – that was the human thought in the heart of the Creator! That is the true life in grace. To seek the place in life where from the widths of worlds the divine voice could speak in *that* way to us, means, to allow Christ to live in oneself.

And our doing receives the consecration of Christ when it seeks the way of the white dove. In the Middle Ages there were knights who carried the image of the white dove by their saddles. As Grail Knights they fought against evil and harm. *In* us the white dove lets its shining life ray out and continue its sublime flight with calm divinely pulsing wing-beats.

Thus our day becomes Christ's day. The more our everyday, our quite normal day-to-day existence resembles the day of Christ's Baptism, the more we become Christian. *Christ becomes our day,* Then each of our days foretells a great cosmic day to come.

The seer John saw this great approaching cosmic day. He saw *heaven opened* over the earth. The earthly sun no longer shines but God himself in his glory becomes humanity's sun,[3] and shines amongst them, 'Glory to God in the heights!' And there was a city built according to the measure of an angel sounding in sacred rhythms and harmonies.[4] *The Son has become the world,* over whom God's revelation lovingly rests. Jerusalem means 'city of peace'. 'Peace on earth.' And in the city nothing impure any more (Rv 21:27). *People in white garments,* in kingly-priestly service before the Highest. The 'good will', the Holy Spirit.

One day a time will come. To work for it with each of our days, is the life of a Christian disciple. To take Christ really seriously means to create every new day of life resembling the great cosmic day.

Not a twilight of the gods, a downfall of the gods, as the ancient Teutons prophesied, but the rising of God's revelation. Not a sentence of death in Hades, the land of the shades, as the

Greeks saw, but rising above this the divine kingdom of peace and grace. Not nirvana, for which the Indian strove, but work in God's illuminated world.

The early Christians ended the twelve Holy Nights on January 6 with the day of Christ's Baptism. Out of the Holy Nights they emerged into the *Holy Day*.

Paul's Damascus experience

People of the East call Damascus the most beautiful of the four Paradises of the earth, and it was before Damascus that one of the most significant events in the spiritual history of mankind took place. Paul was making his way there, his mind still overflowing with hatred and bent on designs to destroy the followers of Christ within his nation, when suddenly a light from heaven shone around him.[5] So mighty was its working that Paul was overpowered and sank to the ground.

We know today that there is not only the light of the external world that physics know and measure, but that when higher realms of experience are opened to human beings, there, too, they experience light. It is more than a radiance sent out by what is taking place within the soul, more than a mere mingling of the realms of experience; moments there are when one breaks into the realm from which light comes and where it is present in far greater power and with far more intensity of reality, so much that the light of the outer world is but a feeble reflection of it. The light that Paul perceived is a light of untold power, and it is at the same time uttermost purity, radiant holiness and divine wisdom.

Christ is there, and fills for a moment Paul's being with a majesty and a glory of light.

The greatest events of life, however, are by no means so filled with happiness as we might expect. Out of the light came a voice, breaking in upon him from every side, 'Saul, Saul, why do you persecute me?' (Ac 9:4). Such voices come not merely from without; they are from without and at the same time from within. They are not audible to the outer ear; it is as though man himself had helped to utter them, and yet they are reality, more real than all besides. As if in flaming light the whole life of Saul shone before him and surrounded him on all sides. Persecution of the Christ – that is what it had been! For Saul it is as though the voice sounded not only in his ear but pierced with sharp knives into the very marrow of his bones. It is what is called the Guardian of the Threshold. Paul's own being in all its antagonism to Christ stands before him like an angel with the flaming sword barring the way to Paradise that is yet so near.

But now Paul's true being comes forth, the being that has ever waited in the depths for Christ and is now called by Him. Like a hero it comes forth out of its chamber. 'Lord, what shall I do?' (Ac 22:10). That is the Paul that thenceforth goes through all lands like a whirlwind and wins the world for Christ; the Paul who says, 'Not I, but Christ in me'; the Paul who is determined 'to know nothing ... except Jesus Christ and him crucified' and risen again (Gal 2:20, 1Cor 2:2). The man of will in Paul begins to stir and finds utterance in the new will of his life. And all the hours of his life from now on are the consequence of this one hour.

The hour that Paul here experienced stands with inexorable certainty before us all. If it does not come within our earthly life, we shall surely meet it after death. In that hour when our earthly body falls away – and what else is death but this? – behold, the light is there wherein we see our life, and of what nature it has been. More deeply than we have ever thought it, we shall then *feel* the truth of what has been told us concerning the higher world.

With a clarity from which there is no escape we shall see how near, or how far, our life has been from Christ. Christ will be there before us as the judge of all the world, as our judge. Deep in the innermost heart of our being, as it lies there open before him, we shall behold how every loveless word, every lingering in the paths of indolence, takes its place among the evil deeds that fight against Christ and that would seek to prolong the cursed deed of Golgotha. 'They will look on the one they have pierced' (Jn 19:37). We shall see how we ourselves have been busied in piercing the living Christ with our evil deeds. Much of our life is a persecution of Christ.

But if man thus beholds his life as it appears under the aspect of eternity, as it appears in the light of the judge of all the world then there arises within him like a prayer a new will that can become the seed of a better life.

If we contemplate the experience of Christ that was granted to Paul at Damascus, we see how it was prepared in Paul's own life. We see again before us the time when the witnesses laid their garments at the feet of the young man named Saul. With intense vividness the scene is painted for us in the Acts of the Apostles. 'All who were sitting in the Sanhedrin looked intently at Stephen, and they saw that his face was like the face of an angel.' But, 'They gnashed their teeth at him ... they covered their ears and, yelling at the top of their voices, they all rushed at him' (Ac 6:15, 7:54, 57). If we read the whole context in the Acts and we will readily observe that the scene has a vivid pictorial character not to be found in the earlier chapters. How is this?

Two wanderers are walking together along the roads of Asia Minor. One is telling the other of the great hour of his life. Again and again his companion questions him on all the details of that momentous hour. With deep emotion of soul he relates the whole event. Luke listens to Paul; Luke, who later compiles the Acts. His account, as it stands in the Bible for the centuries to read, is an undying memorial of how deep was the impression made upon Paul by the death of Stephen.

And in the great hour of Damascus Stephen came again; he was present there. We recognise in Paul's experience the three last sayings that Stephen spoke. 'Look, ... I see heaven open and the Son of Man standing at the right hand of God.' 'Lord, do not hold this sin against them.' 'Lord Jesus, receive my spirit.' (Ac 7:56, 60, 59).

Now Paul sees the heavens opened and the Son of man standing at the right hand of God. And he is overwhelmed with the sins he has committed. But the prayer of Stephen is fulfilled by Christ; for truly Christ has come not to lay his sins to his charge but to heal him of them. Paul himself becomes a new Stephen: Lord Jesus receive my spirit – not now in death, and yet in death, in the death that leads to a new *life*.

Stephen had need to die that Paul might become. When in long past times great buildings were constructed to stand for all eternity, an ancient faith demanded that a human life be sacrificed and be immured within the walls; and in like manner we repeatedly find in the lives of great prophets of God that a sacrifice has been offered up for their future greatness by another who dies early in life. Luther would not have become Luther without the death of his friend Alexis. Thomas Aquinas endured the pain and shock of having his sister struck dead by lightning at his side. Indeed, even the early death of John the Baptist was a sacrifice was needed for the furtherance of Christ's work. Such unconscious sacrifices – may they rightly be demanded? When in the life after death, the wonderful hour came in which it was revealed to Stephen how his death had been of service to the new and young Christianity, will he not have said, 'Yes' to it?

In our lives, too, are sacrifices that we have to bring on behalf of others. And in the heavenly future, moments await us too when our eyes will be opened to behold their meaning.

How did Stephen come to this 'working together with Christ'? The three sayings of Stephen are in reality the words of Christ, changed and yet the same.

'I see heaven open.' Christ said that to the thief on the cross: 'Today you will be with me in Paradise' (Lk 23:43).

'Lord, do not hold this sin against them.' Christ said the same of his own enemies: 'Father, forgive them, for they do not know what they are doing' (Lk 23:34).

'Lord Jesus, receive my spirit.' With these very words did Christ himself pass through the portal of death: 'Father, into your hands I commit my spirit' (Lk 23:46).

The words are not spoken by Stephen in imitation, they are born again from within his soul. Freedom in his own 'I' and union with the 'I' of Christ are here combined in a wonderful harmony. That is the mark of the true disciple.

But note the three sayings of Christ on the cross are reported by Luke and not by the other evangelists. Do we discern the hidden meaning of this? We cannot for a moment today entertain the thought that Luke invented either the account of Stephen or the report of Golgotha. But the deep experience he underwent as he listened to Paul's narration of the death of Stephen became for him a new power of vision; he was able to read at the cross what the others had not read. He was 'inspired' to behold what happened at the cross, with an inspiration that he owed entirely to what he had himself suffered.

Our experiences on earth can become for us eyes and ears for future revelations. And this is so most of all with those that are darkest and give sorest pain. So it was with Luke; so it was too with Paul. In the secret depths of divine wisdom and goodness, there is a providence within us that sees far beyond the immediate hour, far beyond even the single life.

Through Stephen there came to Paul the call of Christ from the cross. And Christ calls us too in every word that he spoke.

Within every word of Christ lives the whole experience of Paul at Damascus.

When we let one of the great sayings of Christ work upon us, there dawns within it a world of light. It is not the single experience that we may have from the saying that is important; it is that in the saying a divine light sheds its rays upon us, a divine world draws near to us. We are repeatedly amazed at the fullness of light that is as it were imprisoned in such a saying of Christ, and that waits for the person who is ready to receive it. Christ has left his whole kingdom upon the earth – in his words.

But as within every saying of Christ is contained the 'light from heaven' that shone around Paul, so too in every word is heard the voice of Christ, 'Saul, Saul, why are you persecuting me?' That is the bitter experience which cannot be spared us. The new world that comes towards us out of such a saying of Christ stands before us like a stern reproach. All the opposition to the world of Christ that is inherent in our nature, such as it has become, rises up into consciousness and becomes for us the hard reality in which we must live. A new world stands before us, so near and yet so far, raised high above our reach. We feel right down into the very bones of our body how opposed we are to Christ. 'Saul, Saul, why are you persecuting me?' We see that we stand with our life on the side of the opponents of Christ, and yet we would be among his friends. Well for us if we discern this, if we recognise this unquestionable truth. For then we receive beforehand what we must otherwise undergo after death. We do not 'come into judgment' because we have met Christ in life.

And it is not 'too late' when now another 'I' stirs within us, 'Lord, what shall I do?' This better self, this new will – this also is contained in every word of Christ. This 'I' of Christ is the secret that lies deepest in every word He spoke, and it can come to us in every word. Like a garment of fire he holds it out to us: the new 'I', the Christ-'I', that is all Christ, and yet all we ourselves.

People of old would have said, 'A Christ-initiation awaits us in every saying of Christ,' Our thinking, our spirit, receives thereby the light of Christ – and our whole life appears differently when we turn upon it the Christ-light of one single word of Christ. Our feeling, our soul, receives the essence and being of Christ – although at first in such a way that it feels its own distance from him. Our will, our being, receives the will of Christ – and a new world opens up within it.

That the experience of Paul at Damascus is truly an experience of Christ will be still more clearly revealed if we look out surveying the far reaches of earthly evolution, if we look far back to the beginning of mankind's history and far, too, to its ending.

The Bible places before us the beginning of the history of mankind in a mighty picture: Paradise, and therein the Tree of the Knowledge of Good and Evil, and the Tree of Life. Is it not all there again, before Damascus?

The shining light from heaven: Paradise begins to dawn for man once more.

The voice that reveals to Paul the truth concerning his life: the Tree of the Knowledge of Good and Evil.

With the flash of the spark of will, 'Lord, what shall I do?' the Tree of Life reaches down its fruits to mankind and begins a new life within.

And from the mountain height of the primordial beginnings we look across to the mountain height where the last things are revealed. John, the seer, beheld them. The gates of Paradise swung wide on that Sunday hour on Patmos. And what did he behold?

Christ himself, the Son of Man, mankind's true Paradise and heavenly realm. 'His face was like the sun shining in all its brilliance.' 'His eyes were like blazing fire.' (Rv 1:16, 14).

But a world-judgement more terrible than man has dreamed of comes forth from the lips of this Christ. The judgment of the world and the judgment of mankind in the utmost earnestness – these are the vision of the future that comes to the seer through Christ. The Tree of the Knowledge of Good and Evil is set up upon the earth.

Then, however, the new heaven and the new earth come down. 'I am making everything new!' 'The glory of God gives it light.' The name of the Lamb 'and his Father's name written on their foreheads.' The Tree of Life gives them of its 'twelve crops of fruit, yielding its fruit every month,' and 'God's dwelling place is now among the people ... God himself will be ... their God.' (Rv 21:5, 23; 14:1; 22:2; 21:3). 'Lord, what shall I do?'

Among mankind the world over, the promise has now been felt for many years that we are approaching a new Christ-age. The experience of Paul at Damascus will come again, at first for a few and then for an increasing number of people. Is this an idle prediction, or is it a call to us to hearken from Christ himself?

Passiontide

The washing of the feet

When a solemn festival begins, all the bells are set ringing. Thus a festive peal is rung in John's Gospel (Ch 13) before the Washing of the Feet is performed, the deed with which Christ introduced the sublime Eucharist. Let us listen to the heavenly peals that seem to call the angels to the celebration.

> It was just before the Passover Festival. Jesus knew that the hour had come for him to leave this world and go to the Father. Having loved his own who were in the world, he loved them to the end. The evening meal was in progress, and the devil had already prompted Judas, the son of Simon Iscariot, to betray Jesus. Jesus knew that the Father had put all things under his power, and that he had come from God and was returning to God; so he got up from the meal ...

Christ rises from the great earthly meal of mankind. Not for enjoyment did he come, but to bring the sacred revelation of serving. He laid aside everything, except the one garment which he needed with which to serve. Do we see the transparency of the account? He does not speak, he acts. We behold as he completely adapts himself to human arrangements when he now does one thing, then the next, as servants do. So he fulfils deed for deed the meaner service like a sacrament.

Voices are raised in the group of disciples, who wanted to see Christ differently. The whole world should be laid at the feet of Messiah – and now he goes and washes the feet of the others! Peoples should be subject to him – and now he bows down and fulfils the meanest service. The disciples had all wanted to fight for him – and now they sit and accept simple help. 'You shall never wash my feet.'

But Christ restrains, 'You do not realise now what I am doing, but later you will understand.' Golden tones from yet greater heights are blended in the chiming bells.

> 'Do you understand what I have done for you?' he asked them. 'You call me "Teacher" and "Lord," and rightly so, for that is what I am. Now that I, your Lord and Teacher, have washed your feet, you also should wash one another's feet. I have set you an example that you should do as I have done for you. Very truly I tell you, no servant is greater than his master, nor is a messenger greater than the one who sent him. Now that you know these things, you will be blessed if you do them.

And then after the betrayer has gone out – not only of the room but out of the picture of humanity:

> Now the Son of Man is glorified and God is glorified in him. If God is glorified in him, God will glorify the Son in himself, and will glorify him at once. My children, I will be with you only a little longer. You will look for me, and just as I told the Jews, so I tell you now: Where I am going, you

cannot come. A new command I give you: Love one another. As I have loved you, so you must love one another. By this everyone will know that you are my disciples, if you love one another.

Let us feel with the deepest powers of our soul what *love* this picture contains. It does not please itself as a feeling but a conscious 'I' is carrying free deeds down from peaceful heights.

Judas is there, too. But he cannot cloud the shining revelation in any way. We forget that he is there. 'Love your enemies' (Mt 5:44) is shown just in this, that it does not notice him or react to him, but in word and deed includes him. Only finally after word and deed does a warning bell sound.

A sacred fragrance is shed abroad from this love and fills the whole house where they sat. Whoever breathes this fragrance is in heaven; he is embraced with the life-giving air of a higher world. He feels breathless and his heart weighs heavy when he is obliged to live again on the earth, but yet in truth this need not be when he breathes this sacred air from within and lets it stream out.

We see Christ walking around and celebrating this love as a Eucharist. In deep festal mood and yet in modest simplicity he raises up the simplest earthly deeds to divine worship and fills the simple earthly deed with all heaven's glory. Highest holiness streams into lowly daily work, into the toil of the despised slave. Earthly walls fade away and over the meanest earthly deed stands a luminous temple.

It is only from the soul that heaven can so burst open over the earth. The moment we drink the spirit of this love, heaven begins to shine around us for our fellow human beings.

Do we behold the 'I' that is active here? Like sunlight it sets itself no bounds and yet rests securely within itself. It does not assert itself and yet is mighty in consent. It does not force its presence and yet it reveals itself triumphantly. The inspiring goodness of a human 'I' that is simultaneously Son of man and Son of God, strives to flow in our blood.

Through this 'I' we can *see God*. Without a shadow of condescension this sacred kingly gesture reaches down from above and lifts us to itself.

The history of Christianity has sometimes shown an enthusiasm for humility. One can understand such a feeling. But that kind of human experience is quite unaware of the high dignity that is now lent to man. We feel that Christ himself purifies us when we give ourselves up to this heavenly stream. 'You are now clean!' Here is love. Here is God.

Our heart feels what life might become were we really to serve such love. Lowliest life would be flooded with a super-earthly light if each day could tell of one revelation of such love in some simple deed for which life always offers opportunities like the Washing of the Feet, unnoticed perhaps by human beings, but not unseen by the angels. In that moment we would be one with God, and that moment would be changed into eternity. In that moment God would call us his true son, his child: Christ would call us his brother and all true Christians their friend.

Scourging

The gospels report in a single sentence, 'Then Pilate took Jesus and had him flogged' (Jn 19:1).

It took millennia upon millennia until it was possible for the fullness of the Godhead to dwell in a human body. A temple was built that had never existed, neither before nor ever afterwards. A body, out of which *'I am the life'* could be spoken, stood amongst humanity. This body in which all the spirits of the heights could find an earthly home walked on the earth and from his mouth the proclamation was true, 'heaven is here.' This body was destined to be eaten by humanity, not as they habitually eat, but in a spiritual meal, as it is in the worlds above, in a receiving through which people are prepared for a spiritual kingdom – and that yet pierces through all the forces of their earthly body and re-constitutes them on the earth.

But now this body was bound that it could not move. It was stretched out that it could not protect itself. And scourging lashes, the feared penalty for recalcitrant soldiers in the Roman army, rained down one after the other on the body. The Roman overseer watched that the executioner was not overcome with sympathetic weakness. He would have then to pay for it by suffering the lashes on his own body. The most noble body was mauled by brute force. Certain soldiers more used to rough treatment than Jesus Christ piled on such relentless lashes.

Humanity, this is what you have done!

And blood flowed from the swollen back. It is the purest blood that ever flowed on the earth, until now preserved as the most costly fluid of the earth in the confines of that noble human body. Now it runs unnoticed on the ground, as if millions of years had not waited for such a stream of life. This blood – thousands awaken to life when they experience but an inkling of this blood from the words of Christ. They experience then for the first time what life is. Blood will become in the future the re-enlivening draught of mankind for all time. But how cruelly humanity seized this blood!

This hour is unimaginable. Everyone who wants to become truly human should pause and stand still before it. A profound silence emanates from this event, even in the gospel. As if the picture waits without words, awaits those who wish to behold it.

Before this picture everything caught up in itself is released in holiness. The saints of past times, who had taken themselves out of the sufferings of this world, come shocked from their caves. Astonished they look at this most Holy One who gives himself to the most terrible brutality. Here a new order of holiness arises and begins its path over the earth, taking up the struggle for the earth.

The lashes which Christ suffers originate from the selfsame power which God himself gave to humanity. And God knew that people would turn against him, and he knew what he wanted to do against it – suffer victoriously. It is the recalcitrant 'I's of the people themselves who hit back against him – and he takes them all into his redeeming life. The motionless peace in which this occurs, the enlightened victory of love that proceeds from this dominant peace – this is the strongest healing draught against all misdeed that we can drink in this life.

We speak of our opponents' 'needling'. It could be 'crushing blows'. We are stronger than them when we have the courage of the Christ who stands there. No man indeed had ever thought this most divine idea, that the victory over all evil is triumphant, enduring suffering. In this one thought we recognise God.

And only someone who is united to the greatest source of strength can hope to be victorious. We see the greatest strength there at the martyr's stake.

Mankind has needed centuries to understand that a god can be struck and hurt. But then, it felt that the deepest secret of the world had appeared, that at last and in reality the highest God himself had spoken, quite differently from what people could ever have expected. Now human beings recognised that no truer picture for the highest God exists than this: that he allows himself to be abused throughout the long history of the world and still carries peace in himself from which the victory of love breaks forth.

When we carry that picture in ourselves, we feel – it is an initiation. We receive a new understanding of the world and a new power to overcome the world, as in the early initiations. Now for the first time we stand properly on the earth. We no longer live away from the earth. We also not only look for the beauty of the earth. We stand right within the overpowering might of evil. And we know that the lord of this world – in that case the representative of the Roman Empire – can do nothing else but hit out against the truly divine: he would bring on his own destruction if he did otherwise. We experience ourselves bound to an inexorable necessity, like the One bound at the stake.

Indeed, we also know that we become more sensitive to these blows the more the divine lives in us. If previously we could be indifferent to some evil words and some evil deeds so we notice now in everything the blows of the fiend of destruction. Indeed, we feel them directed against us, also when they do not reach us personally, the more our destiny unites itself with the divine destiny.

This is the new, extreme gravity of that which previously one had no inkling. Our destiny becomes Christ's destiny. We increasingly experience that only a divine strength which comes from heaven can be equal to these blows. But we also receive this strength. It is provided thus. We feel the divine suffering only as far as we carry the divine strength in ourselves.

Thus our destiny merges in reality with the divine destiny. Our personal complaints become unimportant. We add new suffering to the old, but for this the old personal complaints fall away from us. And for the new suffering comes the strength for a deepest bond with the divine being of the world. We survey long ages. We focus on farthest aims. We are united with what becomes in the world through Christ. That is *the* peace.

In older times initiation was gained only through pain. But not pain which came from the habitual course of life, but through pain that one took on of one's own freewill. In the Christian life the suffering that we suffer *through* others is superseded by the suffering that we suffer *for* others.

What happened there at the martyr's stake indeed also happened without ceasing throughout the whole life of Christ himself. If we only read the Farewell Discourses (Jn 13–16) and the uncomprehending interruptions of the disciples which are like whiplashes – there he stands at the martyr's stake receiving all the lashes and allows everything to sink into the sea of his deep divine peace.

People always seek consolation for *their* suffering. For this Christ also had words and deeds, and always has. But those who unite themselves with *his* suffering seek him at a level higher than those who only need him in their suffering. The life-spring wells up of unceasing power for overcoming the world from the place of the martyr, where Christ once stood.

The crowning with thorns

Sleeping Beauty or Briar Rose is an ancient, well-known fairytale that contains the secret of the thorns. Once there lived a princess. She knew nothing yet of the tower in which there was a spindle. She was happy in her father's house, but over her cradle the gods hold sway. Twelve fairy-godmothers surround the slumbering child. The dangerous step of a thirteenth entered into their cosmic plan. On her fifteenth birthday, the day of awakening on the earth, the princess is suddenly hit by her fate.

The tower in the fairytale is an image of imprisonment in the earthly body and within it earthly work is waiting for human beings. For a hundred years the princess is lost slumbering under thorn bushes and everything that was once alive around her dies. A deep sleep fell over the old, one-time glory of the world. Then according to the holy will of the gods, the prince approaches ...

In these pictures the divining spirit beholds the history of the human soul on the earth. Conventionally dressed, the old fairytale lives with us today. But do we not see the eyes of the mysteries shining through? The ancient wisdom of myths hid itself in fairytales for children, to be able to survive in withered times. But the eyes disclose the daughter of the gods.

Behind this fairytale we can see the Teutonic saga. Brunhilde sinks through the sleep of thorns in world-slumber as in Wagner's Ring cycle. Thus she awaits her deliverer.

Humanity today is not used to seeing the feeling world of sagas and of fairytales in connection with the hard facts of world-history.

There before the tumultuous mass of people stood a figure with the crown of thorns on his head. How the disciples must have felt if one of them had seen that spectacle from a distance. As if the heavens would fall down. As if the fallen heavens buries everything under it which was holy for them.

They had hoped to see Christ in the radiance of highest glory, the heaven-sent Lord of the World. And now the billows of rage broke over him. But he stood upright ...

Soiled, tormented, helpless, dishonoured, he is howled at by the destructive hate of the people. A dreadful play of mockery by the mob occurs unhindered in front of the rabble. But he stood upright ...

The head, whose forehead was like a throne of the heavens, whose eyes shone like a loving sun, was torn and blood overflowed. The head, in which lived the lamentation for the distress of humanity, was surrounded by scorn. The hands that had healed and exaltedly pointed to heaven were bound and had to hold a feeble reed-stalk. But he stood upright ...

If a disciple in this hour had been able to remember the story of thorns in the Bible, he would have had a first distant glimmer lighting up the darkness of night. The ground of the earth 'will produce thorns and thistles for you ... until you return to the ground, since from it you were taken' (Gn 3:18f). That was the human lot since the time of Paradise.

But one day out of the thorn-bush a divine voice spoke. Its words come to a demure, lone man in the wilderness, 'I AM THE I AM ... this is my name forever, the name you shall call me from generation to generation' (Ex 3.14f). Was the reason for man's existence on the earth, that one day he could receive the revelation of the I AM from the thorn-bush? Under the thorns of suffering and the thistles of sin, man should himself become an 'I', that he might become the recipient of the highest divine revelation of the I AM. God's revelation, his revelation, awaits man even in the thorns that the earthly ground produces for him. To hear, even Moses had to wake up under the thorns of misery and the thistles of fiendishness.

In this hour the meaning of the banishment from Paradise blazed up. The thorns began to shine. Since this hour a hidden light awaits in every thorn-bush on our earthly path. 'It is I' and leads us out from the thorns to the true 'I'.

And now the third thing comes, the fulfilment, The I AM himself appears on the earth. He goes directly to the thorns as if to his chosen plant. He plaits it into a new crown, to his kingly crown. Thus he stands before humanity, 'Behold, the man' (Jn 19:5).

Now your thorns, O earthly ground, are on his forehead. Now your sufferings, O man, twisted into a king's crown, are on his forehead. All your complaints – behold them – are the twigs from which you have to twist a new crown for yourself. A different crown flourishes from earthly pain than the golden crown of the kings of old, the crown of the true I AM.

The thorns of the ground first drank Christ's blood. Let your thorns drink blood, Christ's blood. You behold only the spikes.

Christ knew more about the suffering of the earth than the Buddha.

Behold also the purple mantle. Who knows from which Asiatic king it was torn as booty! But if we can behold colours then in this purple a whole story is spoken. Kings really wore purple in olden times not only because it looked fine and was costly, but because it spoke of that which they should be. The prophecy of purple is also fulfilled in Christ. The love in which Christ lived enveloped him like a shining magnificent red garment. In the colour of his own blood the shining light of love lived around him. That was his kingship. That is also the kingship of man, in which the kingly meaning of the earth lives.

And behold the bound hands, which defenceless carry the swaying reed. In the bound hands immense strength is gathered. From his own strength man is no longer anything. But the reed in the bound hands points to the new sovereign strength that will come completely out of the spirit.

'Behold the man.' This saying is certainly not spoken by chance at this hour by the Roman imperial prefect. Scene by scene we see *the* man before us. Around his head he bears the wisdom won from suffering. And all true wisdom is endured suffering. Over his heart he bears the kingly cloak of streaming love. All genuine love is devotion and royalty at the same time. And he is bound by the hands to serve a higher will which he awaits from above. He received his human will for this reason, that he offers it to the heights above. 'Behold, the man.'

The more we take in this picture, the more human we shall become. But we must remain upright among the blustering crowd.

This picture becomes an 'initiation experience' again. And it changes within you, as it changes from John's Gospel to the Apocalypse. In the former the crown of thorns; in the latter the raying light of heaven. Here the miserable earthly cloak; there the heavenly cloak with the girdle of stars. Here the weak hand with the reed; there the seven stars in the right hand and the sword of the spirit, which is governed by the Word.

A friend, who in a blessed hour was allowed to behold Christ, related that the stars in the hand are alive, spreading forth light. Cosmic forces proceed from the hand that received the seal of the piercing nails. Behold the Man.

The seven words from the cross[1]

Every striving Christian looks up to the *cross* this week in deepest worship. It is the time when in past centuries the saints retreated day and night to relive the sufferings of Christ, to die with him so that they might resurrect through him. Our Good Friday festival today is not to imagine the literal martyrs of the flesh and to imitate them. But we would like to learn to go through these hours with his soul. If only the profundity and the greatness of the grand Christian ages were closer to us!

We look up to the cross and try to receive the revelation of Christ. The seven words from the cross stream down to us. And right through them the Lord's Prayer rays forth again. A transformed Lord's Prayer; in them we recognise a Lord's Prayer glowing with deeds.

'Give us this day our daily bread.' It was a prayer of most gentle modesty standing over earthly existence. Whoever takes the spirit of this petition walks in freedom over the earth, just touching the earthly, purified of worldly entanglement, but full of humility integrating into the conditions of the earth. The same spirit greets us again from the cross, as the One dying spoke the simple words, *'I thirst.'* Once more he takes the most modest refreshment from the earth in order to complete his work awake and clearly; he takes it – asks it of his tormentors. Why do we allow the consecration of all earthly gifts to escape us, which flows from the memory of this purest earthly contact?

'Forgive us our trespasses as we forgive those who trespass against us.' Now we hear him praying on the cross: *'Father, forgive them for they know not what they do.'* An unequalled force of mercy streams from this saying into the world. And yet this mercy streams from a sure knowledge. 'They know not.' Indeed, it is terrible what is committed here, and there would be no possibility of mercy *if* they knew what they were doing! This conviction is breathed into his being, the truest faithfulness towards the highest, and the overflowing of mercy which blesses our existence amongst humanity.

'Lead us not into temptation.' He who taught this prayer himself wrestles in the blackest night of temptation. *'My God, my God, why hast thou forsaken me?'* And if this saying did not exist, the struggle in Gethsemane tells through what realms of darkness the Saviour of mankind had to find his way. And the spirit which enveloped and accompanied him right through every frightening darkness was none other than the God whom the Psalmist addresses when he felt deserted, *'my God'* (Ps 22). None other than the God addressed in the Lord's Prayer, who will lead us *through* temptations, is nevertheless boldly and in complete trust, borne in the heart: 'Lead us not into temptation.' From this hour our soul is permeated by the strongest will to purity in deepest connection to God.

'Deliver us from evil!' Humanity's whole distress calls out in this prayer. Like an innermost sigh, helpless, confused humanity groans upwards to heaven. The same mouth, however, which spoke this saying from the deepest misery of the human race, may now speak on the cross: *'It is finished!'* His own struggle of suffering, dark as an abyss, is fulfilled; the salvation of lost humanity is fulfilled. Victory rays down from the cross. The majesty of victory glows in the inner place of the 'I'.

Yet before this happened, behold Christ once more on the earth. What of the divine will still remained unfulfilled? The disciples are scattered. His last earthly possession, his garment, is being gambled away. No one wants anything more from him. No one can receive anything more from him. The end of his earthly life stares him in the face. Yet two people are still standing there who feel they belong to him, a mother and a disciple. A 'last will' sounds down from the cross. It is the will for the human community, through him, in him. The will, which really had always been his ultimate, highest will. *'Woman, behold your son ... Behold your mother.'* Still in a last whisper the divine will is fulfilled, which will be revealed over all earthly humanity. Then they see him disappear into heaven. *'As in the heavens, so also on the earth'* might have sounded over the fulfilment of his will.

Another saying was heard earlier by someone else who also still wished to be blessed. *'Today you will be with me in Paradise.'* *'Your kingdom come'* – now it is coming. It stands with opened doors above him. And with his friend the sinner, the Saviour of the world enters the divine kingdom.

Mankind heard the last saying of all from the One departing. *'Father into your hands I commend my spirit.'* It was a great flowing back of the whole life into the first word of the Lord's Prayer, *'Father.'* Once again the highest name sounds from his lips. Once again with his death he fulfils the petition: *'Hallowed be your name.'* His word, his life, his being pronounce once again the name of all names in sanctification. So he goes from the earth up to God – so as to live on the earth always.

When we see the first three petitions of the Lord's Prayer, when we see the whole Lord's Prayer as a deed of prayer rising up from the cross, shining with soul. It is an immersion in all the consecration that our thinking, feeling and doing can possibly receive.

The seven sacraments beneath the cross

One only needs to observe with open eyes the deaths which occurred before Christ and those that occurred after Christ in order to see everything.

Let us take as the greatest deaths those who died before Christ, the death of Buddha and the death of Socrates.[2] In festive solemnity the 'perfected one' goes to his rest. The memory of it belongs to the most glorious treasures of mankind's experience. In blessed freedom the wise Greek took the cup of poison. 'You wish to hurry me? Watch out that I do not slip away from you!'

But indeed one who has love for these great men can recognise how completely different tones sound forth in the kingdom of Christ.

There is Stephen. As death approached him it is as though for him the heavens were torn open. 'I see heaven open and the Son of Man standing at the right hand of God' (Ac 7:56). Christ is there and opens the heavens for him. It is a *baptism*. Death it is who leads him to this baptism. Death could do no more to hundreds of Christians than open for them the full glory of the divine world.

Bishop Polycarp (AD 69–156), as he was threatened by death, only responded, 'I have served my Lord faithfully for 86 years and he has never done anything bad to me. Should I now my Lord forswear who has done nothing but good to me?[3] He made of death a festival. He made of it a confession. He made of it a strengthening for himself and everyone else. It was like a *confirmation*. Death could have from him, and many with him, nothing other than accompanying him to a festive blessing.

The Czech theologian Jan Hus (*c.* 1369–1415) was a passionate disputant. But as the death by fire approached him, he had but one thing – a humble confession of his sins and an earnest prayer for forgiveness. Death came and showed him his life unveiled, and showed him the only Redeemer of his life. That was the deed of love which death could still fulfil for him, nothing more besides. Thousands of others fared similarly in the kingdom of Christ. Death is transformed into its reconciling Father Confessor. What has become of death through Christ!

Thomas Aquinas (1225–1274), the greatest spirit of the Middle Ages, lay dying. The priest came to him with the consecrated host. The sick man could raise himself once, indeed stand up and standing freely received the body of the Lord. Christ in body and blood had been the heart of his theology. Now death was able to do nothing more than to make for him the *Eucharist* the most solemn festival of life.

In the North a holy monk lives whose wish it was to translate the New Testament for his Anglo-Saxon people. Only John's Gospel was still lacking Chapter 17. Then the Venerable Bede *(c.* 673–735) became ill. With utmost exertion of strength he translated on his sick-bed verse for verse. Still one verse was missing: 'Now this is eternal life: that they know you, the only true God and Jesus Christ, whom you have sent.' The monks assembled around the bedside. The scribes waited. The dying man whispered with his last strength the missing words. 'Glory to the Father and to the Son and to the Holy Spirit!' Then he sank back, in death.

To how many has death given the strength to test their work, to complete their work, offering their work to the divine world itself. In death they have been *ordained priests* of their life's work.

And death has joined the hands of others in comradeship as nothing else could join. They recognised the link between them just as death stood between them. Now for the first time they spoke and did their best for each other, just because death was come. It was like a *marriage,* greater and more solemn than any other, under the blessing hand of death. Thus the disciple John had at his passing only one phrase on his lips, 'Little children, love one another.'

Let us speak of one more death. As Francis of Assisi (1181–1226) felt that he should die, he began to sing. The bishop, in whose house he was living, came to him. 'Francis, you can't do that, a saint can't die like that! But the saint, who throughout his life had humbly fitted in with his seniors in the Church, felt himself now free from authority. He sang and sang, and whilst singing he passed over. What was there still left over from death? Death must himself approach and give man the consecration to a *higher* life. Death brought man a *last anointing*. What has become of death through Christ!

Whoever reviews all this, sees how death is changed through Christ. Death walks consecrated over the earth, and has become a helper of Christ. Nothing is left of death in the inner being of those who belong to Christ. Indeed, we have seen death who like a priest may celebrate all seven sacraments. The old destroyer of the human countenance has become a serving priest of Christ.

Easter

The dawning of Easter

For the vast majority of people, the Easter experience is to begin with like a dull dreaming. The Easter message has reached the ears of mankind, barely touched its soul, and certainly not its 'I'. This becomes overwhelmingly clear if one looks for Easter pictures, or for music that could sound in the Easter celebration. Where in art does the resurrection live as something more than a faint notion? Where do the Easter trumpets blare? Where do light and air become permeated with awakening qualities? Where does this new and radiant day triumph? Where are the dead roused from their tombs?

Easter is not yet here.

In a few chorales, however, Easter does breathe its first breaths. Goethe must have felt this when in *Faust* he describes how something that has died within us feels it is summoned by the Easter bells, how a buried seed of life is stirred by the Easter hymn. Perhaps Goethe in his youth had experienced this in the poet Klopstock.[1] Klopstock was one of those in whose soul the knowledge of Easter lived.

It is very remarkable how the secret of Easter in Goethe's *Faust* is broken up in three ways and becomes increasingly dark. *The Easter bells from the church* touch the ear but not the soul, or at best only a still dreaming, slumbering soul.

The Easter sun in the morning rouses only a dull stirring and an urge to go out.

This is also the reason why the quality of *Easter life in John's Gospel,* to which the spirit is drawn, cannot yet speak to people.

The first experience remains dull, the second external, the third completely lost in dreams. The result is the tragedy of Faust.

But we can nevertheless glimpse in Goethe's *Faust* what Easter will one day become for humanity. The contemporary level of human awareness of Easter is, as it were, preserved in Goethe's *Faust:* yet a prophecy of Easter to come is nevertheless apparent in the background.

'Pursue ever brighter and more beautiful thy course, O Easter sun!'[2] Do we realise that our ordinary everyday light is dead and dull compared with the radiance of Christ's light shining in our daylight? It is proclaimed in the Easter prayer in the Act of Consecration of Man that the earth breathes and lives in the spirit-radiant power of the sun. People will come to feel the resurrection within their very own breathing.

Sound, however, is the first aspect of Easter in Goethe's *Faust.* Did Goethe feel that it is in music above all that Easter will be proclaimed? Even today one can receive the impression that ever since Christ's resurrection there is a gentle sound in the air as if a thousand Easter symphonies lay dormant awaiting the day. This Easter sounds forth not only in vaulted cathedrals but in the universe itself. Once again, the Easter prayer in the Act of Consecration of Man speaks of the rejoicing of the earth in its airy element.

But the New Testament, too, will undergo resurrection. Easter is present especially in John's Gospel. But only if we have resurrection in our blood will we understand it. For Goethe's *Faust* it still lay in the tomb. When Easter's hour arrives life will break through with a roar. Mankind's Eastertide is not yet here. The enormous force of the resurrection awaits its day, till it bursts death's barriers from within. The dead 'came out of the tombs ... and appeared to many people' (Mt 27:53). This will take place among us, the 'living'. This, too, is spoken of in the Easter prayer in the Act of Consecration of Man. Blood itself begins to rejoice in the Risen Christ.

Eastertide for humanity as a whole, however, has barely arrived as yet.

What does Easter mean today to 'Christians'? A slight hope of life after death, but even this is gnawed at by doubt and often sustained with difficulty.

The way things are with us can be clearly revealed by looking at our own death. When death is no longer a black curtain behind which an unknown world awaits us; when it has become light behind the curtain so that it dissolves into transparent veils through which a world of divine radiance is revealed; when the prospect of immediate death fills us only with feelings of shame about our past deeds, with concern for the welfare of those we are leaving, but is incapable of causing us a moment's anxiety about ourselves; when our state is like that of Francis, who was one of the few who knew about resurrection, so that unsuspected sounds of jubilation are aroused in our soul; when the Buddha in us, staring mournfully into the kingdom where death holds sway, has been overcome, when the whole background of this realm is filled with awakening music, when nothing remains of death but a friend who teaches us to distinguish between the important and the unimportant, a friend who has become the inspirer of our life's work; when from the innermost depths of a new being the song bursts forth, 'Where, O death, is your victory? Where, O death, is your sting?' (1Cor 15:55); when this has become our constant basic attitude to life so that we live with the feeling that we have at last historically done with death – then we know what

the Apostle Paul was after when he wanted 'to know Christ ...
to know the power of his resurrection' (Phil 3:10).

A yet higher sphere presents itself to us in John's Gospel.
'I go to the Father'. One may detect the complete overcoming
of death that dwells in such words. Here there is no more
triumphant jubilation, for the adversary has disappeared.
'I – go – to the Father.'

In the Greek Orthodox Church people greet each other on
Easter Day with the words 'Christ is risen!'

Easter will have come to exist in mankind when we
inwardly bring this greeting towards everyone we meet. The
joy which is alive in the Easter assurance is the *force* asking for
a new relationship between human beings. The summons to
resurrection that resounds for a person's own resurrected being
is, even if not expressed literally, the *spirit* of a new relationship
between people.

We can become 'revivalist preachers' in a higher sense than
the expression has ever been used before, The Easter person
who sleeps shrouded and entombed in others is bound to hear
the call, 'Christ is risen!' through everything we do. It is *the*
greeting with which all people inwardly greet one another once
Christ becomes a human experience.

How far away from this we still are! We are dead with
'a reputation of being alive' (Rv 3:1). About 'life' we know
nothing. We carry around a grave within ourselves, a grave
in which, however, something lives that is able and wants to
undergo resurrection.

What a solemn feeling there must have lived in human beings
in the early Egyptian initiation chambers when the pupil was
placed in the coffin and put to sleep; when the hierophants
caused images of a divine world to appear around the sleeper
until he was awakened after three days and walked about

among mankind thereafter as a messenger from higher realms.

Waking in freedom on a higher level is something we ought to put back again into our life. Could not our praying sometimes – or even always – resemble this deed of consecration? We leave this world. We die to it and make our way consciously and freely into the realm that we enter after death. There we hearken to what Christ's heavenly helpers – not priests – have to say to us. They will have much to entrust to us if only we become still enough for them, become quietly reflective and peacefully prepared. If we lift ourselves up then we undergo resurrection. *We* are the new initiates who leave our temple to re-enter the world.

We have not yet reached this state. But every prayer, every meditation can be death and resurrection. Christ's death-resurrection wants to find its home in our everyday life.

The account of the raising of Lazarus (Jn 11) becomes more transparent the more often we read it. Just as the whole universe is in the atom, the whole of the gospel begins to come to life within us when we become Christians. Can we not find Mary and Martha living as forces in our soul standing before Christ; the mourning so lacking in hope, the conflicting doubts? Does not something of the weeping Jews stir within us, and the waiting and willing disciples who do not yet know and do not yet believe?

It is possible to experience the story of Lazarus in its full sense only when we feel Christ coming straight towards *us*, when we feel him in his overwhelming greatness immediately before us, when his grave-shattering summons forces its way into the tomb of our soul, 'Lazarus come forth!'

This Christ is a quite different Christ from the Christ who was proclaimed to us earlier. And mankind's future rejoices within us towards him. His 'works' make their way into the narrow confines of our being – a complete, holy story, not only consolation for his death but the power of his miracles and the light of his resurrection as well.

Indeed, we even hear within our own being Christ's prayer, 'Father, I thank you' (Jn 11:41).

If what Christ has given us so far – the Bible, his gospel, his life and deeds – does not even come to life within us, how shall he give us even greater things? He wanted to give us greater things and promised to do so.

How should the Easter services be arranged? Music, music! But as yet mankind has no resurrection music. We do not yet hear the resounding air. The choirs of angels are not yet heard. It should be the kind of music which makes the grass prick up its ears and the mountains begin to sing; a music brought down from a quite different world, a music in which the dead awaken.

A sermon? – but one who has undergone resurrection should give it. Every word should speak of 'new creation', should shine like a ray of sunlight from the Easter sun. An echo of resurrection-fanfares should sound forth from each tone. Every raising of the hand should be like the life-spark of a new creation.

A play? But it should include Christ's path to Lazarus' tomb, the quite irresistible power of the vanquisher of death. Graves should be smashed and rocks shattered. And in the midst of this a voice should call out so that everything dead should sense new life.

We have the Act of Consecration of Man. The time will come when it will be embedded in such music, in such a sermon, in such a play. But it is already Easter. Christ is laid in the grave of bread and wine, and arises therein. Mankind will see him shining forth. Christ is laid in the grave of a human body and arises within it. People will sense his creative activity, how he builds his temple in a new body and with his music fills it with a new blood.

It is here that Easter comes about. Here Easter can be brought about – if people are ready.

Our awakening in the *morning* can become our teacher about the Easter festival. Awakening can become increasingly like resurrection. We fetch ourselves back from a spirit-world in which we have lived. But in the things of the spirit that we bring back with us, and which play around our awakening body, there exist possibilities of spiritually awakening the earth to which we now return. Light shines less earth-like now. The wide world greets us as if surfacing from eternity. People are given to us anew and approach us as divine thoughts. Each morning can bring us nearer to an inkling of an Easter morning. Resurrection flows around us.

Are other times of the day connected with Christian festivals?

Yes, each *evening* which sinks to a close can become a Christmas Eve for us. Evening after evening the stars sing a song of praise to the Holy Night. Our soul is woven around by the miracle of divine radiance out of which the loving eyes of the Father look upon us. We become children again who 'enter the kingdom of heaven'. Evening and morning turn into day.

Night, however, brings Good Friday and entombment. Although we do not feel it because it is an everyday event, each going to sleep is a little dying. Here, however, we do not see death from the viewpoint of torment, annihilation and disappearance, but from the viewpoint of entering into divine glory.

'Father, glorify me in your presence with the glory I had with you before the world began' (Jn 17:5) – this is also the mood for night and nightly prayer. The stretching out of Christ upon the cross was not only a torture but also a picture of revelation. He was to be spread out all over the spaces of the world. We go through a death every night; may we make an effort so that our sleep becomes more like Christ's death – in all particulars. Christ on the cross forgave his enemies. But he also told his disciples that they should not even let the sun set on their wrath. Even the two last sayings of Christ from the cross, 'It is finished' and 'Father, into your hands I commit my spirit,' (Jn 19:30, Lk 23:46) can cast their divine light over our last waking thoughts before we fall asleep.

The more our going to sleep becomes Christ-like the more our waking up will become resurrection. Easter music and Easter jubilation will seem to sound in the air.

Midday, however, turns into Pentecost. The sun shines strongly from without – all the more powerfully should the spirit radiate from within. The fire that Christ came 'to bring ... on the earth' (Lk 12:49) seeks to become ever stronger when compared to the fire of the sun. And the three miracles of Pentecost could come true in us every day – that heavenly light should illuminate us; that the mighty wind from above should inspire us; that new language out of Christ should pour forth from us.

Beyond Hamlet and Faust to Christ

In the great literary works of mankind the Spirit of the Age expresses its conviction. When the writer's muse becomes the sanctuary which tempts the Spirit of the Age to come forth from the background of existence and tell mankind about itself, then a great moment is reached in the art of writing. Deeply hidden secrets are revealed. The subterranean chambers are opened where the web of time is woven and where the future is fashioned.

Hamlet stands in the graveyard – before him an open grave. The gravedigger throws up skull. Hamlet takes it in his hand and ponders upon it. The riddle of life stares him in the face. His soul is overcome with horror and dismay. He unburdens himself in clever thoughts, but these cannot reach the place where answers are to be found. He flings away the skull. Life goes on – and leads Hamlet to his death.

Do contemporary people recognise themselves here? Can we behold anywhere a truer picture of ourselves? The world about us has become like a battlefield that is strewn with bodies of the dead. People die. Humanity dies. The world dies. That is the sum of our wisdom – so far as it relies upon the knowledge and research of our age. Man lives his life in the midst of a yawning abyss of the past. The earth itself is the grave that he sees before him. Onward flowing time has become the gravedigger, and out of the grave of the earth he also throws up objects to ponder and study. Whatever the research, it is a dead object man holds in his hand. In anatomy it is the human corpse, in physics he enquires into what is dead in nature and in astronomy into what is dead in the universe. The contemporary scientist is eminent at such research. But *life* eludes his methods. He gazes fixedly only upon the empty skull. Clever thoughts are on his lips. Never has thinking been more subtle and acute. Nor has it ever been so inadequate. The philosophers of our age are powerless before the riddle of life and the longings of the human soul. At times man's dismay and dread break out in a pessimism that looks forward to a universal death such as Eduard von Hartmann prophesied,[3] or again in a shrill cry of despair such as was uttered by Nietzsche. But then man flings away the skull and turns to 'life' – life, of which he has no knowledge or understanding.

Shakespeare and Goethe are to one another like the world and the human being.

Goethe's *Faust,* as well as Shakespeare's *Hamlet,* stands before a field strewn with bodies of the dead. Where the world of the senses, the world of outer objects, is spread before the eyes of the Englishman, it is the world of books that the German has around him; but Faust sees also in his world of books a cemetery of graves. 'No dog would wish to prolong such a life!'

Faust, too, holds a vessel in his hand. It is not a skull from which death grins upon him. It is a cup of poison from which death comes to meet him. Fundamentally, it is the same experience. The German looks at everything subjectively, whereas the Anglo-Saxon feels he is face to face with the external world. Hamlet sees the destiny of mortal man in the dead creature of the earth; Faust feels the impulse for suicide as the last consequence of life. He forestalls the philosophies of the coming century. The higher man within us can no longer live. How many a man of our day, even while he follows the very highest in the science and culture of the time, heard a whisper within him of utter weariness of life, to which he has not the time – or maybe the courage – to listen!

Shakespeare's Hamlet is English through and through, and is thrown back into life by life itself. Faust, the German, is recalled by the Easter bells. The mighty past asserts itself and scares away the ultimate consequence that was facing him. In Faust there speaks the promise of his own heart. For Hamlet it is the possibility, the chance, that may yet be given to the objective world outside. The little relic of faith in the heart of Faust is strong enough to hold him in life, though not to hold him in the path of goodness.

As one looks upon these two visions of mankind, one is amazed to see history and the very conscience of the world, through the mouth of these great writers, proclaiming how the Englishman and the German is each incomplete without the other. By letting both come to life within us, we can enter deeply into the mind and heart of our contemporaries. For here indeed we have the contemporary person. When he discovers his true nature, he feels lost and deserted upon the earth. Neither the world of things nor the world of books can hold him. The empty shell of the earth, when he considers it, is full of nothingness, and when he tries to touch it, there is poison within. From the quiet hours of true self-reflection there is nothing to lead him back into life but dubious possibilities without or unvanquished remains of faith within.

Christ at the grave of Lazarus. The tomb has opened before him. He speaks to it – not, like Hamlet, a philosophy, but a deed. And this deed is not, as with Faust, to take flight from life; it is life's own deed of victory, bringing the answer to all her riddles.

Nowhere in all the world can we behold a more sublime spectacle. Christ stands facing death. It is as if he sees before him, in spirit, the whole might and power of death. He sees death with all his host, like a living being. The Christ's spirit-being rises up to meet the being of death, His divine 'I' bursts forth from the depths within, 'I am the resurrection and the life' (Jn 11:25). His whole being is shaken with the tumult of conflict, when he beholds the 'enemy' face to face. 'He was deeply moved in spirit and troubled' – the mighty event surges like a torrent within him and the onset of its power reaches right into the body itself. 'Jesus wept' (Jn 11:33, 35). And so he goes forward, making straight for death, seeking him out of his own castle, in his own rocky grave. The human participants in the event draw back, as peoples of old used to give place when the kings approached one another for single combat. Majesty set over against majesty: the majesty of life confronting the majesty of death.

With an almighty voice Christ calls out his creative Word into the world of death. It is the same voice which the seer John later likens to 'the roar of rushing waters' (Rv 14:2). Death is overpowered. He recognises his victor. He brings the keys of the conquered city, and gives up his spoil. Christ stands before the whole world in the glory and radiance of victory. The sun shines upon his garment of light. 'Father, I thank you that you have heard me' (Jn 11:41).

The Easter chorus in the church held Faust in life. But something coming from outside can no longer suffice for the contemporary person. A new song of resurrection breaks forth from within, from the human 'I'. 'I am the resurrection and the life.' Here lie slumbering all the songs of resurrection for the future of humanity.

Job in solemn hope had promised, 'I shall rise again.' 'I *am* the resurrection,' says Christ.

Socrates, as he faced death, had felt, 'I shall live.' 'I *am* the life,' says Christ.

Victory rests with the 'I' that is apparelled with the divine, that has been united with the life of God.

Is it not as if Christ held the whole earth in his hand like a skull – the empty skull of death – and turning it about, poured new life into it from above? The vessel of death becomes the vessel of the Grail. Not nothingness and not poison, but divine life now fills it to overflowing. 'Did I not tell you that if you believe, you will see the glory of God?' (Jn 11:40). The field of dead bodies becomes the field of life.

Here is no return to life in doubt and perplexity like Hamlet, or in quest for enjoyment like Faust; but a life newborn, born now of the divine. Lazarus comes forth. He is bound hand and foot. He can neither walk, nor be active to do and to make. His head is bound. He cannot see. But he comes. At the call of Christ he had the courage to venture into new life.

And Christ himself, as he turns back once more into life, is no longer the same as before. The experience of death that he has entered into with his friend has awakened in him the hidden Easter power that will bear him back to life on Easter morning. He had first to raise another from the dead in order himself to rise from the dead. Lazarus must rise again that Christ might rise again. A resurrection *before* the resurrection; this is what we behold at the grave of Lazarus, an inward resurrection. Wherever neither Hamlet nor Faust, but the Christ returning to life within a person, stirred with the surging life of a deathless world, there is Easter, there is Christianity.

Christ's radiant glory

We have learned through Rudolf Steiner to take seriously the fact that the spiritual side of man rays around a person as a coloured aura, which not everyone, though nonetheless some, can perceive. Now suddenly the halo appears in a new light. Long ago people with an appearance of light perceptible all about the head, were called saints. Today when a pure person steps into the room impressions still live, though unclearly, that it becomes brighter.

Christ as the divine Son could not have fulfilled his work on the earth in ancient India 7,000 years ago. He would have been too quickly and surely recognised. In those times humanity was unable to see the body distinctly, but saw the spiritual all the more clearly. Steiner often brought the comparison of the lantern that one sees unclearly in a fog, but it is surrounded with coloured rays. The human faculty to behold the spirit directly had to recede, right up to blindness. Perhaps this entails the idea that people who were still demoniac 'recognised' Christ from his radiance. The biblical stories of the possessed can be so interpreted.

Can we learn something about the glory that rays from Christ? Does it mean something for the spirit to know this?

When people spoke to me in confidence of having 'Christ experiences' then usually I asked then about the glory. They always answered, the lightest red. My dear friend Michael Bauer, who exactly on Epiphany – he later pinpointed the day – was blessed with such a light-filled Christ-experience, told this to me on his death-bed, full of reverence.

Matthias Grünewald had the courage to paint the glory of Christ. This courage is not often to be found in history.

For a long time now I have observed this aura as one looks at a painter's conception. Then it occurred to me with the principal colours here – the inner part light, then red, then green – that indeed the same is proclaimed in all clarity in another language, which John's Gospel presents before us as *the* Christian message: light, love and life.

Did Grünewald think of this? Was he one on the track of reality?

One day the picture of Christ as it hangs above many altars of The Christian Community came from Milan. It was copied from the original in the Brera Art Gallery. And, lo and behold, exactly the same three colours are there, inside bright, then red, then green. Only nearer the head than with Grünewald and richer in colour.

Did both painters come to a mutual understanding? Copied from each other? Most probably they had never seen each other's pictures. From where does the agreement come? Would they have had the courage to paint the light around Christ had they not been inwardly sure?

Contemplation dips into this glory once more. Something wonderful occurs to us. These three colours are indeed the colour images of the Father, Son and Holy Spirit. The Spirit lives in the inner light. It is embraced by the red of the Son, who is love. And out of the creative green – does not outer nature reveal this everywhere – speaks the life of the Father.

In Christ the divine Son is present before us. From this background the red dominates. But 'in unity' with the Father and the Spirit.

But where is the blue? We see that the green with Grünewald loses itself in the deep blue of the night sky and the green in the Brera picture is darkened into violet. We can sense deep mysteries of life are revealed.

The painting is a baptism. The colours become word and bear witness how Christ is surrounded by the light of the eternal Godhead: Father, Son and Spirit.

And this is true which we know from spiritual science, that thinking is strongest and most closely connected with the physical body, with feeling more loosely, and the will still more freely. Thus light is nearest the head. Red embraces it. Green-blue surrounds it.

Have such observations a serious meaning? Will not some say, that is quite strange and unacceptable to me?

People of old called the rainbow a bridge to heaven. This saying is to be understood as having inner meaning.

One can raise the colours when they are pure – as in the rainbow, or in the blue of the sky or in the red of the setting sun or in the green of spring – raise them to heavenly impressions!

Thus the radiating shining of Christ is also a 'bridge'. We can behold 'heaven' in it. We can go over into heaven as the gods in Wagner's *The Rhinegold* enter over the rainbow bridge to Valhalla. The deepest inklings of life reach us in such prophetic colours. Colours are the alphabet of a divine speech. When one bathes in them one can receive through them a baptism of light.

Glory to God in the heights
And on earth, peace to men of goodwill!

This song of the angels sounds together with the singing of the colours.

The light within is the glory of the revelation from the heights.

The raying red of love brings the peace down to the earth.

The life-creating green, that comes to rest in the blue of devotion, binds us with the deepest will-forces to the universe.

'In your light we see light' (Ps 36:9).

Ascension

Heaven

Ascension morning. The air was full of the silver sheen of the brightly shining sun. The body, still resting, awakes from sleep, in well-being from the gift of refreshment. Then in the mind a still voice was heard. 'Do you want to behold heaven?' I pull myself together. I am aware of an angel standing behind me. I did not see him, but I clearly felt his presence. He appeared larger than I and was completely of light. It was as if he took into himself the best of my being. Lucid peace – one cannot describe it in any other way. Only when my soul was thinking of clear peace was he present. That mood was like a body in which he dwelt.

When he spoke the spirit felt at first only that the angel wanted to make himself known. Then one had to become quite still to grow receptive. If a revelation then came from him it had to be received with one's own being, not just with thinking, as though to catch the moment and oneself help create a garment of words. But these words were necessary and clear. When the soul had become a quiet mirror, the words came out clearly like a picture of the sun in a calmed lake.

I awaited the angel and gave him, not my hand, but my whole being. Slowly my soul was filled with a fine spirituality. *Spirit* awoke in all the realms of soul. It was as if the soul-space was filled with invisible light, which was full of love and life, as the world originally was, all shining and loving. It appeared as through the angel himself. One could only have access when one inwardly said yes to him. Otherwise he disappeared. 'Is that heaven?' I asked the angel in reply. 'Wait!'

Minutes passed. Or was it longer? The feeling of time ceased. It appeared as if heaven itself must make ready the sense organ in the soul in which it can be revealed.

Then the moment came when I felt I should put a question. 'Where are the dead?'

I heard worlds opening. Though I 'saw' no individual, they were there. A billowing of human incalculable longing, struggling, suffering, striving. When I wanted to take hold of them they flowed near and retreated. Homer's description of the shades surrounding Odysseus in the underworld scurried like a memory, as they flowed hither and thither in billows. A world of voices that want to speak and yet cannot speak – not in our speech. A fullness of human feelings of every sort, but all on the spiritual plane.

Again I felt I would not come further if I did not ask again. 'Where is my mother?'

Then she was there, quite near, as though she had already been waiting long. As I became receptive to her being, she said, 'I have accompanied you much more than you know. Why have you not thought *more* of me? The warmth of my love was a fragment of heaven meant for you.' And I felt the enveloping warmth with which her love enfolded me. So near? I thought. Why do we think so falsely about the 'dead'?

But I could not limit the angel's permission to one person. 'Where is my friend?'

Then I perceived him, how – like a tree spreading its branches to the sun – he had all his soul-organs turned upwards. He had been a thinker on the earth, a grave, painstaking thinker. He had not denied heaven, but could also not find it and sought it often, deeply stirred. Now he turned with all his power and force to the world of light. For a moment he looked down. 'Why do you disturb me? I have much to make up. We will meet again, when you yourself have heavenly tasks.' I left him there and sent him a strong surge of friendship as he turned upwards again.

'Where is my teacher?'

What came now was a surprise. I saw what a human spirit means for heaven itself when earthly things are thought through and raised as far as heaven. Already on the earth he had worked to the point where heaven itself lit up in earthly things and earthly thoughts. It was like a precious stone extracted out of the depths of the earth and cleansed to reveal the sunshine it bears in itself. It was as if this precious stone was now brought into the sun and through it the heavenly inhabitants could behold themselves in the strength of the earth and the beauty of the earth and see a *new* heavenly radiance in it. Thus did the teacher's spirit shine in the higher realm. 'Then the righteous will shine like the sun in the kingdom of the Father' (Mt 13:43). These words were suddenly present. How differently the words of the gospel sound in heaven than on the earth! Yes, in truth, as the sun shines on the things of earth so that they are lovingly included by the transfigured sun, so heaven and earth are in communion united in such a human spirit – the earth returned to heaven, heaven radiating in new power.

'But where are the others – those far from God?'

The angel became grave, but peaceful. 'You will see more when you have become stronger,' he said. 'And more redeeming,' he quickly added. I tried harder. Out of the deep voices were urging, imploring, longing. But they were not audible to me. Iron law prevails. A thousandfold agonised struggling against a hidden light that could now no longer be denied, was perceptible. Not without hope but far, far removed. How far mankind still lags behind! Can one bear it when one sees it? Can people thus live, as they do, when they have no inkling? What patience the World-Father possesses, to bear all this in himself – and to wait – and Father-like in holiness to guide upwards through all darkness? All earthly pain disappears in a puff of smoke when one divines the world-pain preparing for heaven those souls lost in sensuousness and selfishness. It was difficult to behold and difficult to look away. But other things were required at this time.

'Where is the world of the angels?'

A pause ensued. Then worlds of life seemed to well up. Unending ranks. The heavenly sons of God? But why do I receive the impression of white dresses? There are no garments here! But there is that which speaks outwardly of white garments. A world of purity which is promised to our longing feelings when we see people clothed in white! And now I understand for the first time why one says the angels sing. They do not sing, they resound. Their being resounds. From their soul-being the thanks of the creature sounds up to the Creator without ceasing. So that is the song of praise of the angels! A many-thousand-voiced rejoicing, always changing and always there, not perceptible to earthly ears and yet filling all heaven. They look upwards to the eternal working of God, beholding immeasurable things that still keep their secret from us; they are ever again kindled in the heart from divine worlds of revelation. They live in their joyful thanks as we humans live in our bodies. Their work is radiating joy.

But I felt another secret. Palm trees appeared in the spirit. Now for the first time I understand these palms. These spirits are themselves growing, burgeoning life on a higher level, blooms of Paradise. Consequently the helpless painter, the beholding creative spirit of man, puts palms into their hands. Their world is white garments, sounds of praise like harps, life of Paradise far removed from death! You look into such a world when you see angels.

'May I behold a 'Spirit of Might'?' I had always inclined to these beings, to the 'authorities' as they are traditionally translated, ever since I learned that the biblical name was no empty phrase. And now I had keep asking questions, for I myself was asked: What do you ask?

The world which now appeared was staggeringly great. 'What are you doing among us, you human child?' came the question from this world.

'I want to have a sense of you, so that I might work better on the earth.'

Then they tolerated my presence. One felt oneself in an exalted spiritual workshop. In these spiritual beings was a creative world-might reaching into form. But they held sway high, high above human creating. They fashion like the sun's radiating strength. If we think of human breathing, varying a thousandfold according to the human 'I' in which it lives, if we think away everything earthly from it and only retain the spirit, and if we think of the world-fashioning forms creating out of this spirit of breathing; then we have an inkling of this world in which they live. It was exactly as if one of these spirits took me myself, like a sculptor takes a clay figure in his hand, looks critically at it, presses and forms it to see if perhaps something might yet still come out of it.

I had ceased long ago to ask, where is all this in fact? I had learnt that realities exist that lie far above the world of 'where', and are yet so real that the word 'reality' first finds its meaning at all, that facing them the earthly reality is crude, hollow, sleepy. Earthly matter is only like the reflection of what true reality is. Now I got to know the word 'reality' in a new sense; in an ever higher and stronger sense reality is the being of these worlds. Full of might, to them on the other hand the thinking of earthly scholars appears as a toilsome, lame, groping in the dark, handicapped by lameness; the works of the earthly artists appear like mere stirring in a dream. We sleep – they are awake. Awake and working in bright, shining versatile spirit-existence and spirit-activity. But we are only able to acquire an idea of their creating from the side turned towards us.

'May I approach a Spirit of Wisdom?'

Again it was as if we must raise ourselves through wide realms, or as if man must first discover more delicate chords within himself on which these beings may play. The human being is the harp of the universe. All beings of the spiritual world wish to sound in him. But the harp is sunk in the earth. It is not *on* the earth, but sunk *in* the earth, so that now the strings are silent and hardly a soul can imagine what shining musical sounds wish to sound on this heavenly instrument crushed to death by the heaviness and dust of earth.

'What are you doing among us, you human child?' came the question from this world.

'I wish to approach you to be able to serve you better.' They tolerated my presence. A much higher world still. Human breathing wanted to cease. This kingdom moved and shone in purest light of wisdom. Here wisdom is no longer human thoughts, the suffering of experience, the maturity of life. Here is wisdom – as in our world we have the earth. Imagine the air in which we breathe were a thousandfold myriad-shaped wisdom of life; imagine the sky which we behold above us was raying knowledge of God in immeasurable fullness; imagine the human beings with whom we live, inhabited not bodies, but exalting shining spirit, moving in manifold versatility;

imagine that light were wisdom and this wisdom were in itself as rich as our whole world, only much purer, more splendid and spiritually alive – yet what are unhelpful human thoughts and fretting human words! Out of God's profound thoughts these beings look down upon us. They are themselves God's profound thoughts weaving in the element of wisdom's being, full of tranquillity, most spiritually delicate, penetrating and suffusing all things.

'What may I behold of Christ?'

As the word 'Christ' sounded, it was as if the whole of heaven were changed into singing. The greatest divine deed has been achieved through him. The whole of heaven shone for joy for the deed only he accomplished and which only he was able to do. The joy was so close that one felt the angels are rejoicing *within me.* As if heaven became visible and audible throughout one's own glorified body. Somewhere, from some hidden spring healing streamed, so strong and pure that the lungs were purified and the heartbeat made sacred. Man breathed in spirit-air of undreamt healing power. And this healing was a gift of bliss from the divine goodness. It was so divine that one spontaneously said: people cannot yet understand this nor bear it yet. Through centuries and millennia they must be educated through the proclamation of Christ before this miracle of goodness can be in them. But then Christ lives in them. One felt the heartbeat of the Father-God like a breath of life of this goodness. One's own heart wanted to beat with the life-pulse of the World-Father.

When everything was covered in festive garments, he himself was revealed for a holy moment. He appeared in human form, as the God-man, as the man-God. In his head lived countless wise ones. let them shine his light. He gave to each a beam of his wisdom and this was the 'new life' for that person. In his heart lives the Helper and Healer of humanity. His blood began to flow in them and this was their divine life. In his hands lived mighty heroes and saints, miracle workers, who, in his name wanted to accomplish unheard of wonders on the earth. His whole body was like a great house, completely open and free for those who wanted to live in it. And this was his true church, those who had found in him their true dwelling. In every breath of life he gave them – himself. He lived in them, and they in him. He breathed in peace and breathed out goodness.

And it was remarkable as though my whole being since the beginning had waited for him and was 'fulfilled' in him. As though through long aeons of time secret master-builders had been building so that Christ could dwell in this 'I' and in this body. For he walked in majesty towards the 'I' as though to his temple that he himself would now transform. And the body begins to glow and the blood within, as if mankind now joins the ever-continuing Lord's Supper. His temple and his meal: that is Christ. Now mankind can join with the song of the angels. Now they themselves have become a voice.

But the angel did not allow me to spend longer alone with Him. 'If you would really behold Christ, then you must also see his opponent!'

In that moment a completely different spiritual kingdom arose. If I would breathe at all in this kingdom, I must think *highly*, be spiritually *exalted*. Spiritual nobility. The spirits, as though adorned with diadems, looked down far removed from earthly misery. Ever and again the elusive spiritual nobility. As though each had to bear the spirit in himself and to live his own importance in it. 'Self-glory' – the earthly expression acquired a living meaning here.

'The devil?' The angel turned my gaze downwards. And I saw how the kingdom below opened into the hard, cold human selfishness. That was at the same time the devil's earthly home.

But above there was the light-holding, light-bearing, being of light. Lucifer – thus it seemed to me. The proud spirits were magnificent – perhaps they should be so? But cold! Completely removed from the living fire of love. The great 'seduction' of humanity. A feeling of gratitude came over me in an odd way, that I was allowed to see this kingdom. Now I know where it creeps in on the earth! Now I can combat it consciously!

I walked among these spirits as a spirit of another sort, as a spirit who can no longer bear this absence of Christ. Then – like a single mighty spiritual view – the great Tempter himself stood before me. 'All this I will give you if you fall down and worship me' (Mt 4:9, Lk 4:7). That is really how he speaks when one beholds him. Always. He had spoken thus not only to Christ; essentially he had already spoken thus to Adam. It sounded almost as if he said: When you worship your 'I' in my glory. And when we look at him only for a moment, then it is as if a serpent rises up within us. That is indeed the serpent which seduced Adam, according to the biblical scene. It really is there. It still lives. High, high spirituality and proud beauty – you can have them, but at the price of not allowing distress into your soul, that you allow the earth to go to ruin into the abyss. If this wish stirs in this spiritually high power directed downwards, the will to sacrifice, then Christ is there, and overthrows Lucifer. Can man help in this, by experiencing this spirit in himself – and leading it down?

Cold spiritual splendour, beautiful to look at, seductively beautiful. But no, one does not belong there when Christ has touched us with his breath. I longed for the earth.

Then a completely different world arose like a counter-picture. 'The Earth-Spirit!' He it is. But how exalted! Penetrating intellectuality. All earthly thinking lived in him. Thousands upon thousands of servants with clear, strong intellectuality set up the earth as a kingdom – and forget the heavens. 'The devil?' Now I first saw how distortedly people think about the devil, how they take grimacing, alarming ghosts from the lower kingdoms for the devil and thus deceive themselves of the truth of their earthly plans. The soul was possessed of the immense seriousness of a cosmic struggle which mankind does not comprehend at all. 'The prince of this world' (Jn 14:30) – he was that, indeed. Truly a lord! Not in any way 'the silly devil'. Also the prince of the age – when one looks on the outer surface. How secure this kingdom already feels in human ownership. Great earthly strength proceeds from him. Mankind must have it, I said to myself. A mighty desire gripped me to think with this spirit. Everything was so transparently clear and strong as life. But then it was as if a stony force from the distance wanted to penetrate my brain and enter my whole being. With this spirit one will make bread from stones, I thought. But then bread will become stone – through this spirit.

I looked back to the angel. And now I saw how hard and painful it was for him to look with me into this world at all. Then my soul named the name 'Christ'. And in the same moment it was as if this whole exalted spiritual world crumpled up, its colour faded away. It could not bear the name of Christ. It could not hear it said with special fervour. It was alien to the Christ-spirit, as if out of a completely different world-evolution. But faced with the name of Christ it became stale and was lost in the distance. It was a kingdom that called for a tremendous development – and yet must still pass away.

Far distant, down on the earth, the Christ-statue in Dornach arose before my gaze. There was Christ indeed, walking forward with victorious steps. One hand he raises on high, and under its power of revelation Lucifer falls into the depths. The other hand he holds downwards, strongly warding off, and under his spiritual power Ahriman sinks into the abyss. I could not understand everything in this sculpture at that moment from my own experience. But I had found an innermost connection to it. In truth, out of the spiritual world Christ wants to be *in* us on the earth – and from the earth into the living spirit!

Now I turned quite changed back to heaven. It appeared to me indeed as if I was greeted there quite differently. As one who has gained knowledge of his earthly task. As one who has somehow fulfilled a world-duty. Should Lucifer and Ahriman be redeemed in humanity? Can humanity fulfil something that otherwise no one is able to do? All the worlds appeared to regard humanity as the one being courted, the decisive factor in the struggle for the world.

Heaven, too, appeared quite different. Now I realised how shining spirit-life ruled among the heavenly sons of God like a sunrise. Music sank down from the open heaven. Goodness flashed out of the spirits, like the sun appearing from still much higher heavens. Now one was really within the divine creation.

The 'devil' had helped me to understand Christ. Is he included in God's plan? In God's world-leadership?

I hungered to behold something really great. A Seraph? I did not venture to ask. But he was already there. Only an inkling. But an inkling of a heavenly force for which human words cease. It was as if someone towers up from earth to heaven. I could not see his countenance. I felt as if I had lived much too little in God's eyes to be allowed to look on him. From beholding God his countenance has become sublime, surpassing this world. But the great power of his fire of love I could feel, feel from far away. Nothing of pride, the most purest goodness towards all being lived in this divine sublimity. 'The inconceivably high work.'[1] It was as if this fire-world itself wanted to stir in the mouth of the beholding human being, as if divine fire wanted to live first on his lips. Is this the truth of Isaiah's vision, when the lips of the prophet were touched with the glowing coal of the angel? Was it a kiss of fire from the Seraphic kingdom?

'And the World-Father?' It was as if the Seraph invited me to look through him. He concealed the Father – and revealed him. Yet only the sea of an enormously great divining was there. An echo of very distant singing of super-earthly rejoicing before him, as when waves of the sea festively move, living in light. 'Do you not taste him?' asked the angel indulgently. And the taste of a completely inexpressible goodness met my tongue. All the width and all the depths exhaled fragrance from the glory of grace. 'Our Father in the heavens.' Now this word from the Prayer of Christ became alive for the first time, heavenly alive. I looked for the earth. Nothing more of it was there since the hidden heaven behind it had opened. One looked through it everywhere into 'the heavens'. The veils were so transparent that they themselves had disappeared.

In perfect majesty, however, there surged through the whole universe: 'I am deeply hidden and yet quite near you. I am everything and yet live in you. The heaven of heavens does not contain me, but your life is a breath of my life, too. Let a divining of me be enough for you. You also guard my mystery.' Out of the depths of the world like a beam from an eye, comes a ray from which one can live a whole eternity. Then it led me gently to Christ. 'Behold, this is your Lord. I give him to you.' Music sounded, overpoweringly magnificent, yet at the same time so wonderfully life-inspiring, as if it was the original music from which all music is born: the unity of the Father with the Son! Christ shone, as though surrounded by the purest, strongest light of a hidden sun. 'The Lord of the heavenly forces on earth.'[2]

Earthly gravity was felt ever more strongly. It was as though the body itself had become a being, that now raised itself to speak. 'You belong to me. I have patiently long kept silence.'

'But I have not left you at all. You cannot yet bear heaven for long, to which you also belong.'

Like a flash the being of the body nodded agreement. And I said 'Yes' to it, too, and its earthly wishes.

'May I tell?' I asked the heavens above. It was almost as if a light cloud lay over the heavenly radiance. Like a shadow the memory whisked over to Lucifer's kingdom.

'What is given to man, that is not given to him purely for himself!'

'But to speak directly about it?'

'One may, when your own life approaches maturity.'

'One should', other voices ordained, looking down to the earth as it is today.

'Do what you yourself can carry. No-one should leave the earth without giving of his best to his brothers and sisters.'

'How will they receive it?' Still I persisted and appeared stubborn to myself.

'Do whatever is *good.*'

Like a final admonition came the words, 'Do not forget to tell your brothers that they see only little of heaven when they look through you. For you are small.'

'Quite small!' kindly said other uncountable heavenly sons of God.

'Also do not forget yourself that you will behold a thousand times more when you have become bigger.'

Slowly the doors of the heavenly worlds closed. As if of itself the words came to my lips, 'The Act of Consecration of Man, thus it has been'. And behold, looking back I recognised now what I experienced had been an Act of Consecration of Man. The realm of angels, the great *Word* from heaven. Christ the divine *Offering.* The cosmic struggle, the history-fulfilling *Transformation.* Finally, the divining of a final *Communion.*

I was on the earth again – but with the radiant knowledge of heaven.

Pentecost

Pentecost of humanity

> When the day of Pentecost came, they were all
> together in one place. Suddenly a sound like the
> blowing of a violent wind came from heaven and
> filled the whole house where they were sitting.
> They saw what seemed to be tongues of fire that
> separated and came to rest on each of them. All of
> them were filled with the Holy Spirit and began to
> speak in other tongues as the Spirit enabled them.
> (Ac 2:1–4).

We read the familiar account, and we seem to breathe the
atmosphere of a Sunday school lesson. Can it still have full life
for us today? Can it come to new life?

We let our gaze wander back over the past history of
mankind. We behold the ancient Teutonic troops ranged
around their king. Shields in their left hand and swords in
their right, they advance to meet the enemy. In the forest a
storm is raging. The tumult of the tempest is no mechanical
effect of high and low pressure, but is the noise of battle: they
behold Odin's men coursing through the air. The heroes ride
past them like ghosts. Odin himself towers above them all and
charges forward with a mighty shout.

Awestruck, their hearts beat high. They feel they are akin to the god who lives in the tempest. It is a moment of rising life when they feel a sense of power and well-being. Odin is near. God of strength, awaken our courage! Lead us on to victory!

Quite another picture rises now before our eyes. The Persian High-Priest stands before his followers in the full dignity of his office. He kindles the holy fire on the altar of sacrifice. As the light shines with a divine radiance, so in the soul the flame of prayer glows. Solemn songs resound to the great god who dwells in light. Men of noble nature dedicate themselves to his service. They are champions of light against darkness! Warriors fighting for truth against falsehood.

The mind's eye runs quickly over the history of humanity. Once more, another picture. The prophet of Israel stands before his people. Yahweh has spoken a mighty word to him. He desires to elude it, but it is too strong for him. It burns in his soul, it burns in his limbs and upon his lips. It may be his death. He knows that. But it is also his life. And so he hurls the wrathful message into the midst of the trembling crowd. His enemies come on against him like a roaring sea. The priests shoot arrows of hate from their eyes and their hand clench as if they already held a death-dealing stone. The prophet stands there in his greatness, mighty in sprit. Yahweh is with him.

Once more our vision travels back to the day of Pentecost; and now that great festival of humanity begins to stand before us in the fullness of its life. We behold it as a cosmic event in the history of humanity.

The tempest is there. The world is in tumult, as it did long ago in the days of its creation. New life, new becoming, breaks in upon the ageing earth. In the storm of the worlds the Lord draws near. 'I am making everything new' (Rv 21:5). He does not drive over people's heads as once Odin drove through the

Teutonic forests in springtime. He breathes into them anew the divine breath and they are God-filled. So do they become his heroes, who fight and die and conquer for a new world.

The fire is also there. It comes from heaven. It is heaven itself. It is not lit on the altar as of old. The human being himself has become the altar of sacrifice. Now is the hour for the fulfilment of that mystery of which the sacrificial altar has spoken for thousands of years. People shall go through the world like radiant torches of heaven. 'I have come to bring fire on the earth, and how I wish it were already kindled!' (Lk 12:49).

The word is also there. It comes not to judge nor to avenge. Healing is within it and atonement for mankind. Its voice carries far beyond the people of Israel. Yahweh no longer gives words to people. They begin to be 'words' themselves. When they speak the *Holy Spirit* speaks in their words.

In the east, the fire. In the west, the tempest. In the centre, the word. The Pentecost of humanity.

In the spirit, the word that makes us prophets.

In the soul, the fire that makes us priests.

In the will, the storm that makes us kings.

Pentecost of the world

When we were young children, of all the Old Testament stories none was so strange and perplexing as the story of Elijah on Mount Horeb.

> And the LORD said, 'Go out and stand on the mountain in the presence of the LORD, for the LORD is about to pass by.' Then a great and powerful wind tore the mountains apart and shattered the rocks before the LORD, but the LORD was not in

the wind. After the wind there was an earthquake,
but the LORD was not in the earthquake. After the
earthquake came a fire, but the LORD was not in the
fire. And after the fire came a gentle whisper. When
Elijah heard it, he pulled his cloak over his face.
(1K 19:11–13).

The gentle whisper or still, small voice, we were told is the
Holy Spirit. Elijah could catch the voice of the Holy Spirt,
when as yet it was only a breath.

As we grew older, did we not feel in our soul how Yahweh
was speaking a personal word to Elijah here? Was he not
himself storm and tempest, this Elijah, when he stood before
Ahab and thundered forth the judgements of the Lord? 'As
the LORD, the God of Israel lives, whom I serve, there will be
neither dew nor rain in the next few years except by my word'
(1K 17:1). Was he not himself an earthquake, when the earth
delayed giving bread to the rebellious people, and a fearful
hunger and starvation rent their bodies? Was he not himself
a fire, when his spirit called down the flames of the Lord and
the 'fire from heaven' fell and consumed the burnt sacrifice
and the four hundred priests of Baal? Did he divine in this
moment that someone higher than he would come who should
speak to the soul of people in an altogether new manner? That
God would one day be revealed in a Spirit in whom dwelt the
deep stillness, and thus the mightiest of all revelations, like
the gentle sun in springtime shining on people, thus having a
power that can awaken the depths? Did Elijah cover his face
because he saw himself by the side of Christ?

As the years of our life went on the story spoke with ever
greater power. It seemed to strike the hour of God in the Old
Testament. Upon the same Mount Horeb, where Moses had
heard *what* Yahweh spoke, Elijah, now his brother in God,
heard *how* Yahweh spoke. For he speaks in the inmost being of

man, in the 'I', and his voice is like a gentle wafting that moves the 'I'. So the word of revelation spoke in God's true prophets.

The surrounding nations had a different experience of God. They experienced him in the movements of the airy regions, and in the ecstatic quaking of their own soul. They experienced him in the picture of the visible world and in the work of creation in their own body. But Yahweh spoke with a far deeper solemnity than those other gods. He made himself known in the high places of man's inner being as a greater 'I' that moves and sways the human 'I'. In like manner his prophet did not proclaim him from signs and omens taken from the weather, or from sacrificial fires, or from the entrails of animals; he proclaimed him from the holiest of holies in man. Now at length man stands upon the earth in his full dignity. Within the highest part of his nature he carries God. There God makes himself known in a voice that is no more than a breath and that yet bears divine power hidden within. For him alone man had to live.

Nevertheless, this was not yet the final revelation of God. Storm and fire and word came again, this time in human beings themselves. And that was Pentecost. For the 'I' in humanity had grown strong that it might receive again into itself the greater God, who fills the world outside.

God *was* in the storm at Pentecost; but man was no longer seized by the tempest and borne away he knew not whither; he experienced in the storm the union of outer and inner.

God *was* in the fire at Pentecost; but the fire lived no longer in nature; it flamed up in man himself as a new soul permeating nature and spirit.

God *was* in the earthquake that came from the speech of the Apostles, when the walls between the peoples fell before the word of the message; but this power to make the earth tremble and change went forth from the inner being of man.

Thus the Feast of Pentecost stands before us; the greatest hour of the new covenant answering to the greatest hour of the old, bringing to it the word of the higher revelation. A reconciliation is effected between the world outside and the world within. Elijah had first to enter into the stillness, that God himself might draw into that stillness and from there win the world anew. What spoke once from the universe to human beings, speaks now from human beings to the universe.

Pentecost of the 'I'

How shall I come to know Pentecost in myself? How shall the storm of the Spirit be born in me, the fire of Christ be enkindled and the speech of God be made a living experience?

We turn our eyes to Christ. Did he not himself speak of the Holy Spirit? Did he not confidently promise him to his disciples? We read over again Christ's words of farewell; can we find in Pentecost the fulfilment of the promise of the Holy Spirit?

These is no other way; we must try to read these words as if we heard them for the first time, as if we ourselves were present in that hour of parting. We must hear Christ speak as if he were resting his eyes upon us, as if his voice were directed to us.

When we read in this way, how the words begin to ring! There is a music in them, as if the sounds of a golden harp were borne to us over distant seas. Waves of living light move through the words. These words are truly the home of the soul, which we have always sought, though we knew it not, and which is now seeking us. For the first time in the depths of our being, we feel what 'home' means.

We dive into the sea of life that comes flooding into the kingdom of earth from invisible shores. Health streams through our body and through our whole being. Now we know what health is, and that it is for us not only wholeness but holiness. Has our life ever known a more blessed moment than this? With a like gladness must the earth rejoice when, after the long dreary weeks of winter, the spring sunshine bursts forth and all the wonder of spring lights up for the dead world.

There indeed the Holy Spirit is present. He is in Christ. He proceeds from Christ. Christ sends him to his own. I too belong to them.

But *fire?* Was not the baptism by fire something altogether different? We return to the words of farewell; is no mention to be found there of this fire? Where is it, the fire of Christ?

We catch the glow of a delicate spiritual light. 'As the Father has loved me, so have I loved you. Now remain in my love' (Jn 15:9). We have to turn our gaze upon Christ alone, and devote our whole soul to him; then we shall feel how a living fire descends to us from above, finding a new dwelling-place in our head and in our very self, spreading a glow throughout our being. 'He will glorify me, because it is from me that he will receive what he will make known to you' (Jn 16:14). Must it always be so tempestuous as at Pentecost? Or was it then not as tempestuous as we think, only the mighty picture making a tempestuous impression? Could we but know the 'fire of love, creative of being.' The primal fire from which this world was made and which comes to life in us anew! Now we understand why next to the word 'love' there is always the word 'joy'. Love raying outwards, shining within as joy – that is the living fire of the Father of the World.

But the *language of the Spirit?* Once again we listen to Christ's words of farewell to the disciples. Sacred words meet our ears. 'The Spirit of Truth.' 'Guide into all truth.' Indeed, we shall not behold this Spirit as he is until we feel that he is *the* truth. *The* truth concerning the world. *The* truth concerning all human beings and their well-being. We must indeed first find that language in which we can speak with other people;

in outer as well as inner speech. And indeed, in this Spirit I speak as human being to other human beings, I know that for each single one I have access to that language in which their true human nature comes to them. We carry the true world-language within ourselves. All the peoples and nations can gather together and receive health and healing if Christ really speaks within me.

And the *storm?* 'He will prove the world to be in the wrong about sin and righteousness and judgement: about sin, because people do not believe in me; about righteousness, because I am going to the Father, where you can see me no longer; and about judgement, because the prince of this world now stands condemned' (Jn 16:8–11). 'They will put you out of the synagogue; in fact, the time is coming when anyone who kills you will think they are offering a service to God' (Jn 16:2).

Not in peace, but in storm and tempest will the Holy Spirit come. And we have to learn how he himself is storm. When we see how from now on we have to live from above, how we have no longer a support from below but must be led and guided from above; when we begin to see how he lifts us out of everything that is old, and yet through us would bring a new breath of life into the old; when we give ourselves up to the storm and do not ask anxiously as men did at Pentecost: 'What does this mean?' (Ac 2:12) – then we see ourselves as storm within the storm! Then the might of a new creative power surges through our being. Such a life of freedom may be far from peaceful but it is the only way for the world, through ourselves, to become new. Truly the storm of Pentecost is in us, too, though at first it is only the stirring of a feeble breath.

We have experienced Pentecost and as we give ourselves up to it we learn more of its power to fill our life. Christ has become Pentecost. Now we know where we can find storm and fire and the language of the Spirit. The Spirit of truth: that is the universal language that unites all human beings.

The Spirit of love: that is the cosmic fire that descends upon us from on high.

The Spirit of judgment: that is the storm that would move within us.

And this Spirit grows increasingly individual; it increasingly takes on for us the character of divine personality.

And henceforth our relation to the earthly world, too, is changed. When summer thunderstorms come, they remind us of the storm that would fill our being. In thunder and lightning the spirits live who summon us to battle. When the rays of the sun begin to burn, then we feel how the cosmic fire seeks the response of the fire in our soul. The angels of the sun would dwell within us, even when the outer sun's rays grow cold. And when in this summer-time of the year everyone goes into the country to rejoice together in the beauty of the earth, then we will let the language of the Spirit speak in us; for that is the true earth festival, the true Pentecost of mankind.

Holy Spirit, make us to become human beings! Pour your light into our limbs and let your healing breath waken us to life anew!

St John's Tide

The sun

The sun in midsummer has a dulling, stupefying effect on people. The fullness of light throughout the wide spaces of the world makes one inwardly weak. When people of long-past ages danced their midsummer dances, they themselves changed into dancing rays of sunlight. We feel strong in our body in the summertime, for our physical nature responds to the life and health-bearing influence of the sun.

But people at this time are in danger of returning to a heathen condition. This is expressed in a desire to 'worship the divine in nature'. We have to summon the strongest forces of the soul to remain human in the full sense of the word during the summer.

'What does not kill me, makes me stronger.'[1] The very thing that threatens to destroy people can help to bring our humanity to birth.

During midsummer a wrestling with the sun goes on in the human being. Or rather, we should say, *two suns struggle for the human being* – the outer sun and the sun within. That is how *Christians* feel at St John's Tide.

We are taught at school that Christianity fixed the festival of John the Baptist on the day when the sun's power begins to grow less, because in the words of the gospel, 'He must increase, but I must decrease', a hidden indication was seen of John's birthday. A deep truth is contained in this.

The sun is the great John in the heavens. What John is in the gospel, the sun is in nature. The sun prepared the way for the Christ. For thousands of years people looked up to the sun and worshipped divine salvation in the light. As day by day it rose, bringing for them its message each day anew, they were prepared and made ready for Christ.

Those who were receptive in heart and soul felt a message come to them daily from the sun. It was the very same, in the sublime fashion of history, as the message of John by the Jordan, 'Repent, for the kingdom of heaven has come near' (Mt 3:2). In the pure and healing light of the sun people felt the spirit of the heavens draw near. But they also felt: you are not pure like the sun! You need to be quite other than you are, if you would live in the sun.

And still today, each year at St John's Tide, this warning speaks to us from the sun on its path through the heavens. We feel in all this living light, when we give ourselves up to the weaving rays of the sun, the pure spheres where only what is innocent and blameless can live in the first step from the sun – to Christ.

The sun then speaks to us the second saying of John, 'He must increase, but I must decrease' (Jn 3:30*). The earthly sun grows ever darker with each succeeding centuries; it approaches ever nearer to blackness and final death. It says to us, I decrease. It fulfilled its service to mankind when it pointed to Christ. Coming to the sun to ask of it the question that once the scribes asked John, it answers the sincere and seeking soul, I am not He! It sends its worshippers to Christ, even as long ago John sent his disciples.

And still today, asking further of the sun: who is the Christ? It answers as though from our own soul – you yourself must become fire! Fire from within! There speaks the third saying of John, 'He will baptise you with the Holy Spirit and fire' (Mt 3:11, Lk 3:16). All true and deep experience of the sun leads to the question, *where is the fire that shall fill me with the burning of the Spirit?*

And another voice replies, *'I am the light of the world.'*

Here is the 'I' that streams forth in rays of light; here is the light that arises in the 'I'.

In the past St John's Tide meant: I in the sun. St John's Tide of the future will be: the sun in me.

Every year the sun comes and puts us to the test, to find how strong the light has grown within us. If we succumb to its power and fall into a midsummer dreaminess and sleep, then we are denying Christ; like Peter we are saying, 'I am not his disciple.' If we grow stronger year by year, if we are able to say to the sun: you may decrease, but I will increase, then day is dawning in us, then Christ's word speaks creatively in us, 'I am the light of the world.'

A prophetic saying for mankind is the saying spoken by the blind Faust:

> The night comes on with deeper penetration,
> Yet in my soul there shines a radiant light.[2]

Humanity gazes triumphantly at the expiring sun, which was once the great John of the universe.

The Grail

Many delicate stories tell of it: a little maid, a Sunday's child, finds a miraculous flower on St John's night.[1] Then the depths of the earth are illumined and reveal their golden treasures.

Christ's light wants to arise in our daylight. For someone coming out from the Act of Consecration of Man it can be as if a fine light is behind everything, as if liquid gold begins to flow behind everything visible, as if a new sunlight bursts forth in the being of earthly objects.

Indeed, the more Christ becomes 'the light' in us, the more the depths of the world will be illumined, and the heaven hidden therein will become visible. The forces of heaven are darkened in earth and stone and in everything that we behold. It is sometimes as if they not only light up but also want to speak. But this they cannot yet do for our senses are not fine enough for their speech.

There are inklings also outside Christianity. 'Here the words and word-shrines of all Being open for me: all Being wants to become word here, all Becoming wants to learn from me here how to talk.'[2] What Nietzsche's Zarathustra describes here – even when he felt Christ far from his consciousness – is the experience of St John's Tide. The disciple who bore Christ as the light also found 'the lost word', he also found the Lord's Supper, that awaits prepared for humanity.

But we have to become a Sunday's child, born from the sun. We have to find the miraculous flower, the bloom of heaven that is there in Christ.

Of what the fairytales tell is spoken in the language of the legends of the Holy Grail. A precious stone is brought up from the depths of the earth. It rays forth in the light of Christ. Thus it gathers the true knights of Christ, feeds them with divine food, consecrates them for the struggle for the world.

The Grail-experience is threefold. It leads upwards in three stages.

First *our* 'I' lights up in the head as the holy bearer of divine life. The whole history of the earth has served for this, to 'compose' our 'I'. Now it is there. When we awaken in it and pray to the divine, then we raise the Grail. We have but one choice. Either our 'I' is fulfilled below and cuts itself off from above – then we become a Caesar, small or great, and feel we are as god of the earth to whom all things should be subservient. Or the 'I' is fulfilled in its being born from God, it is left alone on the earth and calls above. Then it is like John the Baptist who is 'the voice of one crying in the wilderness' and is waiting for Christ.

The Grail knight is someone who carries their earthly-strengthened 'I' shining within, because the Holy Spirit is there, the life-blood of Christ as in a divine earthly bowl. Their names are written in heaven (Lk 10:20). They live by what the Grail provides. They are sent out from their sanctuary as helpers of humanity in trouble. Such knights of the Grail exist, even if they never assemble in an earthly castle.

The second stage of the Grail-experience is still higher. *Our whole body* becomes heaven's vessel. The whole earth is indeed present in our body and in it turns back to heaven when the divine in us gleams through it. All heaven waits for us in our body, wishing to become heaven again. We are permitted to carry our body as a world of heavenly forces.

To feel Christ in body and blood means not only to be a Grail knight, but to become the Grail oneself. 'If your eyes are healthy, your whole body will be full of light' (Mt 6:22). Man's body and blood is there to receive the Christ. What the earth brings forth is given to Christ, and Christ gives himself to it. That is the marriage of heaven and earth in the Lord's Supper.

The third stage Grail-experience is that not only man's 'I', not only his body, but *the earth itself* will become the Grail. When angels pass over the earth, then it is another earth. What they behold is not dead stone and dull earth, also not blooming gardens and radiating stars. Everywhere, behind everything, the heavenly countenances of their divine brother shines for them in answer. Everywhere they see higher life that is given from the Spirit. Everywhere they see the divine deeds of offering from God's holy helpers.

That is the truth of the earth. In the depths, however, the sacrificing life of the divine Son streams everywhere 'through him all things were made' (Jn 1:3). He is 'the Word' of the Father, who created the world.

It is the human being who may lift up the Grail that it may shine in Christ's light. It is grace that such a one may know, I am a child of God. A third grace is that one may experience, I am God's helper. Through them, when they completely unite themselves with Christ, they also receive the earth again, from whence it has fallen – the light of Christ, heaven.

The legends tell that the Grail was taken back from the world of the Middle Ages into the kingdom of the priest-king, John. Whoever finds Prester John finds the Grail. He waits in John's Gospel. He asks on St John's Day.

The disciple

The time of the great Christian events that we were permitted to follow from Advent to Pentecost has passed. Now the earth is to give its answer. Its answer is – the disciple whose ideal is the evangelist *John*.

We see him beside John the Baptist. He is like his Christian counterpart.

The *Baptist* proclaims the judgement. The *Evangelist* sees the world-decision, how it really happens through the revelation of Christ.

The *Baptist* awaits Messiah, above whom heaven opens. He is still allowed to see him. The *Evangelist* speaks out of the open heaven that is the Son of God.

They unite in the greatest Christian revelation – uniting prophecy and fulfilment. We see in its fullness the decisive point concerning Christ when we behold them both.

The *Baptist* baptises with only water, but the *Evangelist* is already baptised with fire, with the 'light of the world'.

The *Baptist* speaks: I am not the one! It is he who comes after me: prepare his way! Also the *Evangelist* speaks: I am not the one! He does not name himself; he heard Christ say the word 'I', so he does not use it for himself. But his proclamation is different: I am not the one! He who is *within* me, he *has* entered. That is Christian discipleship.

The name reveals what they both are: *Ioannes* in Greek.

It has not about the meaning, so much as the sounds of the word. This name bears within it the three purest vowels. The sounds express a purified inwardness. We live differently if we bear this name, if we hear ourselves in this name. The *light* of Christ shines in the thinking of John. What met him was bathed in this light. Out of this light he looked out of a radiant castle on to the world, on to humanity and on to history. His thinking was not a dark reflection of existence, but an illumination with the 'glory' of Christ. Evil appeared clearly in this light and received judgment. But a new healing, 'let there be light,' descended on everything that should live. The world recognised itself in light when it entered his head.

Those who let the strong pure vowel I [*ee*] sound in their head, help the birth of this light.

In John's *feeling* lives the *life* of Christ. He heard him speak as no one else had the courage to speak. *I am the life.* Thus John saw him, how he lovingly poured out his exalted being over humanity in the Washing of the Feet. Thus John received him, as in the Farewell Discourses he makes the heavens themselves resound. Thus John beholds him, how through his cross and resurrection he, God himself, walks redeeming through the earth.

Those who bathe their chest in the noblest A [*ah*], who allow the heart to resound in this purest sound, prepare their house for such a Christ-life.

In John's *will* Christ's *love* awakens. But this love is neither feeling nor sweet enthusiasm, but a battle for life and death. It was a battle of life with death. Christ's love may not be called other than that which fights the cosmic battle: love against sin, life against sickness, light against darkness. A strong spirit of overcoming the world wants to live in our whole body, wants to work through all our members. From heart to hand the stream of a new creative will surges.

In the sound O [*oh*] lives the greatest pain, but also the highest joy. From this the deepest inwardness breaks out into the world. Proceeding from I to A to O, we feel the strong force that wants to lead from the divine spirit of the world into the great perfection. We can feel we are contained in this force. It lives in all the activities of our members.

In the German language I*ch bin das* A *und das* O (I am the A and the O) the full sound comes out that governs all world-events.

It is a Johannine initiation about which we speak. The human being begins of itself to create sound. A name is experienced, a new name. In the vowels one's inner life is allowed to sound facing the outer world. In the pure vowels the purified inner nature becomes speech.

And when a human being truly sounds, then the cosmic Word also begins to sound. Anyone who is a 'John' can speak of the 'Word'.

That we are not playing with thoughts should be clear. Divining, we touch on deep world-mysteries that belong to St John's Tide.

A whole world-development speaks out in the three words, *Tao, Taotl, Iao.*

Tao was an ancient word for the divine being. In China, in America, through this word they looked up to the divine being. Yet the I [*ee*] was missing. And humanity had not yet the inwardness of the 'I', or individuality. Consequently, they could not hear the 'I' sounding in God. They were still tribal beings. Instead they felt the *T* outpouring through the widths, *T* breaking through to revelation.

The early pure belief in God decayed in later America. *Tao* became in Mexico small and narrow – *Taotl* (or Teotl).

On the other side of the world, however, the fully human revelation of God slowly ripened. The commandment still existed in Egypt: whoever speaks the word *Iao* should die through the juice of a peach stone.[3] There was a divining, but it was not yet permitted. As God revealed himself in the name Yahweh – as much as the human being could receive was there. Man has become an 'I' so far that the divine 'I' could speak within. Yahweh reaches up to the E-sound [*eh*], which is the specifically human sound: *Mensch, Erde, Welt, Leben* – man, earth, world, life.

Also in Asia Minor the mystery call sounds, *Iao.* In the name *Ioannes,* however, the mystery of humanity became human reality. 'There was a man sent from God whose name was John' (Jn 1:6). Man himself becomes the divine name. The divine name becomes human.

The three great John-experiences – judgement, heaven, and resurrection – are completed in thinking, feeling and doing, as light, life and love.

Whoever fills themselves with light, life and love, whoever is renewed in the purest divine name, whoever repeatedly received holiness from it, themselves receive holiness. They enter into the temple of Johannine initiation, are on the way to the lost word, return again to the Sun-Logos, themselves become a living Johannine festival.

High Summer

Worship in light

The radiant sun has reached its zenith of glory. Into all the wide spaces of the ether its rays shed grace and blessing. Our spirit rises towards the sun. Imbued in reverence our spirit lives in the sun's wide realm of light. We are reminded of our fellow human beings who in long past years, now sunk in silence, were wont to send up to the light their raying souls.

We hear again of the ancient Rishis, teaching their disciples in India:

> The love-awakening light of the enlivening sun, the divine, let us receive it in meditation; it develops in us the power of devotion-filled thinking.[1]

We behold the kingly Zarathustra as he walks up the mountain, feeling above him the majesty of the golden sun, mighty in spirit. He is leading his Persian followers to their sublime divine service.

We hear once more the solemn songs of the sun ringing forth from the temples of Egypt, in Memphis, in Thebes and in Heliopolis. We behold the great pharaoh himself, robed for the festival, standing with arms outstretched towards the sun amid a crowd of reverent souls.

In these three ancient peoples of the earth, the Indians, the Persians and the Egyptians, the thinking, will and the feelings of mankind are raised in prayer to the sun. As we look back into the past, everywhere our eyes rest on people who cherish in their hearts a divine reverence for the sun.

And we people of the present day, are our eyes worthy to look upon God's sun? Day by day its beams shine upon us, but is the sun given to us for that alone? Is not rather our maturity as human beings to be measured by this: how does our spirit think of the sun, in what way does our being live in the sun?

Like an ancient Moses the dying Goethe stood as if on the Mount of the Transfiguration and spoke of the sun.

> The sun ... is a manifestation of the highest Being, and indeed, the most powerful which we children of earth are allowed to behold. I adore in him the light and the productive power of God; by which we all live, move, and have our being – we, and all plants and animals with us.[2]

Sublime and glorious is the temple of the worlds into which we enter, as often as we stand in the light of the sun. Can we hear how divine service is being continually held there, the Father of All letting his own voice be heard? He speaks not in words, but in deeds – in deeds of light. He speaks not of our little questions, but always and unceasingly of the deep and primordial mystery of the world. He speaks not of himself, he speaks *himself.* Into his thousand-voiced activity we enter when we are in the kingdom of the sun. Christ himself has given into our hand the key to this Temple of the Worlds. 'Your Father in heaven ... causes his sun to rise on the evil and the good' (Mt 5:45).

The word of the sun goes forth like a mighty single musical sound. Yet all the fullness of the world is contained in it, if we but knew how to listen. Hearkening to the rays of sunlight, we catch the delicate music of a thousand harps. Singing spirits make themselves known in hushed and gentle tones for the human ear, but for man's spiritual ear in a music of wondrous power. What a paean of joy and exultation is hidden in light! Human souls have always longed to catch the music of this singing. Around them whisper heavenly harmonies in which no single note makes discord. Symphonies of joy flow down to the earth. Who can understand them? Is it the lyre of Apollo that we hear? Is that the music of the spheres?

Love is sounding in the light. Love sings in light. O Man, hear the *Word* of the sun! Receive his everlasting song! The very last of his beams plays golden melodies in thy attic chamber.

The tumult is silent – is it the stillness that comes before a new song? A deeper vision opens to our soul. It streams down to us from the far realms of space, seeking us. We raise our eyes to the heavens; there stands the sun as a tremendous altar of sacrificial *offering,* the original altar of the world. People have spoken of the golden chariot of the sun, but their vision has fallen short; it is not a chariot but an altar that the angels bear daily across the sky that all people may kindle their own being at its touch. Up there above the earth it moves on continually, pouring out its gifts in abundance, sending them on to the earth in mighty surges, yet moving unceasingly in eternal peace and quietness. It does not desire to be anything for itself, but is entirely there for others. The volcano on the earth may foolishly try to imitate, but it can only destroy. Far above lives the altar in divine splendour and glory. If life comes crashing down at times in a thousand deafening trumpets so that the earth cannot endure its onset, it only serves to remind us that the earth cannot yet live in light. Nonetheless, the earth one day will glow in fire – the fire of love.

Who stands at this first altar of the world? The Father of all being; around him a thousand unseen priests of the spirit. He himself brings the sacrifice – he himself is the sacrifice. All this life lavished in untold abundance – it is a sacrifice offered to his creatures. We touch a sacred thing when we touch a beam of light; within it there is the living sacrifice of the Father of all the Worlds; it is his hidden soul. In majesty of revelation the bountiful life of the Father-God is repeatedly poured forth into all the realms of existence, and yet he is throned above, invisible to all eternity.

In medieval times, there was a man who lived beneath the bright sun of Italy. 'Be praised, my Lord,' Francis of Assisi sang:

> Be praised, my Lord, with all Thy works whate'er
> they be,
> Our noble Brother sun especially,
> Whose brightness makes the light by which we
> see,
> And he is fair and radiant, splendid and free,
> A likeness and a type, Most High, of Thee.

We can understand now why people approached the sun with sacrifices. They would speak with it in its own language. They stammered forth what they heard it speak. They felt in their hearts: one can only have converse with the gods when one learns to speak their language, the language of sacrifice.

When John the Baptist, whose soul was open towards God, felt the kingdom of heaven draw near, then for him there was but one word to speak to people, Repent! His call to people to *transform* and repent is in harmony with the word of the sun, the great first messenger of mankind. With the voice of countless rays of light it calls day by day from the heavens: 'Make yourselves clean, pure and radiant. Otherwise it is not possible to live in the divine realms.'

Across all earthly existence the voice of the sun speaks to its children on earth. 'Year by year, I transform the earth again in the name of the Father-God. For one Sun-day I call it back into Paradise. When for one shining hour the earth is turned into a dream of blossom, it is a reminder to you people on earth not to forget Paradise. And then once more I leave you to yourselves. Do you hear my voice? Now *you* turn and change *yourself.* As often as you look up to the sun you steep yourself in the divine power of transmutation.' With an apocalyptic ring the words resound from the far reaches of space, 'Behold, I make all things new! Do you not understand how everything will become changed in you if you give yourself up to the sun? Do you hear the blare of the trumpets? They are summoning the Sun-hero.' In this name in the ancient sacred mysteries human beings were given full and perfect humanity. Man is to work with the sun. The seven miraculous signs of the Christ in John's Gospel are the deeds of the sun transformed into spirit. 'Accomplish Sun-deeds upon the earth; be a Sun-being in the world!'

In far-off times, during the season when the sun stood highest in the heavens, people gave themselves to dancing and dreaming. With shouts of joy they danced about the fires on the high places. Summer is a Christian challenge. It is not our call today to revive the past by setting limbs in motion or reviving old feelings in the heart. From the sun the voice of John speaks to us. Not to tumble in dance but, 'Awake! Repent! Be changed! heaven is near.' To hear in John the word of the sun, to hear in the sun the word of John, is midsummer become Christian. The sun is a John; John was a sun.

Our way has led from Goethe to Francis of Assisi, from Francis to John. And now the path takes us from John back to Christ.

'Your Father in heaven ... causes his sun to rise on the evil and the good' – these words contain far more than a revelation. 'Be perfect, therefore, as your heavenly Father is perfect' (Mt 5:45, 48). In these words does not Christ tell us that the sun will impart to us something of the Father's nature? That the sun will give us *communion*? 'As your heavenly Father is perfect.' 'Father' – that was the very highest holiest word in the mysteries, higher even than the 'Sun-hero'.[4] (As a memory of this is the fact that ordained monks are called 'Father'.) The sun leads us to this newly awakened mystery.

Nourishment of the sun. During quiet hours when we nourish our soul from the sun, we can feel an innermost part within that can only be fed by the sun. We can feel how the sun has been created in order to nourish and sustain that inmost part of our being. The sun feeds as a mother, feeds with the spirit of love, which is the true and ultimate act of consecration.

> It is not the bread which nourishes.
> What feeds us in the bread
> Is God's eternal Word;
> Is Spirit and is Life.[5]

God's eternal Word of light is in truth the bread. Christ dwells within it. Often the bread on the altar has been seen to shine like the sun. The bread of Christ is a food of light. The more people lift themselves from earthly eating to the true life of the spirit, the more closely will they come to feel how in the bread it is the light that nourishes them, and in the light Christ, and in Christ the everlasting Father himself, who feeds them with his own sacred being. The saints of whom legend tell that they were able to live on the host alone are a promise of what shall be for people in the future.

Christ has given back the sun to human beings. Through him we are able to live in the true worship of the sun, our everyday is able to be a consecration of man in light. The old, original word of the sun has died away. People no longer hear and receive it as in the days of the early Indians, Persians and Egyptians. That is as it should be, for the sun must now rise within human beings. From within man the sun shall make all things new, and therewith also the old sun-worship that belongs to the external world of the senses.

Mankind has had two suns in its history. The outer sun has set; its power of revelation is no more. The inner sun is rising in a new glory of revelation. The sun that has now reached the zenith of its yearly path and is beginning to grow less, speaks to us of the Christ-mystery in the history of the world. The old worship of the sun that was for many thousands of years the highest of mankind's festivals, had to die; the sun had entered into human beings and seeks to begin there a new worship.

The Word or Revelation, Offering, Transformation, Communion. The sun still holds its ancient divine worship, consecrated anew by Christ, but it celebrates it like a true priest of ancient time who carries out his work to the end, doing it ever better, whilst all the time his eyes rest upon that which is to come after him and is indeed already there. Christ was there; Christ *is* there, speaking into the ageing world his Sun-Word of the new 'becoming'. 'I am the light of the world.'

With peace in our soul we can now see the sun grow less, with peace we can behold its setting and its expiring – the new sun is here. Those who bear Christ in their soul can feel how the lights of the world of the senses grow dim, for new lights have come. Even the light of man's eye may suffer a gradual darkening during the course of the long years to come. 'In my soul there shines a radiant light.'[6] The blinded Faust divines the world-mystery. And when the priest lifts up his hands at the altar and prays that the light of Christ may shine in our daylight, then all the prayers that have ever risen to the sun from altar or from mountain top are fulfilled in Christ. Before the new day that is rising there, the old sun may sink in peace, turning to darkness and ashes.

'I am the light of the world.' This saying, if we receive it into our soul, will become for us an act of consecration of man.

'I' – therein lives the final *revelation* of all the worlds. Those who hear the sacred 'I' sounding in all life and being, stand upon the highest mount of revelation. The 'I' lies hidden in the very sound of the word 'light'; in the depths of everything abides the great 'I' that speaks with us and reveals itself in us.

'*am*' – when Christ utters the word, he utters a word of *offering*. It is in his death and resurrection that his inmost being is revealed. 'The one and only Son, who is himself God and is in closest relationship with the Father, has made him known' (Jn 1:18). With Christ one can live only in sacrifice and offering. An existence that is not offered up is a stolen existence. Christ 'is' sacrifice, and consequently he helps us also to 'be' sacrifice.

'*the light*' – speaks of the great *transformation*. Transformation, metamorphosis, is the deepest of all the events that take place in history – the change of light into 'I' and 'I' into light. The light would become an 'I': that was the life of pre-Christian times. The 'I' would become a light: such is the life of the centuries since Christ came. This is the divine will that moves behind all world-history.

'*of the world*' – thus this light would become. Here we are directed to the new reality wherein this light would make everything one beneath it, for it fain would give itself to everything. Where this 'world' is, there is the true *communion,* for which all communion at the altar is a preparation and a promise.

Through the light of the sun we gaze into the purest form of worship. The light of the sun itself becomes worship.

Breathing

During the quiet hours of the night when the gift of sleep does not come, I hearken to my breathing. I myself do not then breathe, but I let 'it' breathe and watch the life-movements of this being on earth in whom I live and in whom I am. I watch as from outside and from above. One day it will breathe its last breath. Up to then from the invisible world of air surrounding it, soundless and effortlessly it gathers in each second what it needs to feed the fire of its body. I feel holiness overcoming me through and through. I watch life itself. I recall how the old wise Hebrews felt man received the breath of life from Yahweh Himself. Gratitude for this goes throughout the Old Testament, that Yahweh has planted 'his breath' in man and beast. I recall, too, the wise Indian sages of old, to whom the breath was the being of the immanent God himself, who experienced Brahman also as Atman, as the breath of life ensouling everything. One feels how, allowing such thoughts to move through one's being, one involuntarily breathes more deeply and in a more holy manner. Does not everyone who lives in quiet contemplation or in higher devotional thoughts know how their breathing itself becomes a prayer, a quiet festival of sacrifice? One can do nothing else than 'celebrate' when one breathes. It is indeed not at all oneself – higher powers take creative hold, work through the breathing on our blood, that it flow more purely, fashioning our being through the blood. Yahweh is here ... Atman is here ...

Those who hearken to Bruckner's festive sounds can perceive how they breathe more slowly to appreciate the music; they can then experience why the contemporary person often does not want to perform Bruckner. The long breath of devotion is lacking. People with fine feelings can experience how they breathe differently with each person who sits opposite them, how with one you feel suffocated, how with another the breathing is freed; you experience the intimate being of the other in your own breathing.

In the breathing a huge power reposes over our being. Whoever in an exciting moment keeps their breathing in their power, deep and consciously controlled in themselves, cannot lose themselves. Indeed, a secret creative force over the finest organisation of life is given to you in this breathing. Many people are beginning today to gain a new inkling of this. Many practice it, to win personal power egoistically. Few listen to the true secrets of the world themselves.

In the present age a human being, who still in the centuries of the early Hebrews and ancient Indians was a man of breathing, has become one of nerves and senses. The light appeared then in its divine right after the air. And the contemporary person feels indeed the world-ruling Godhead more truly as the original light than as the original breath. Consequently, the holy worlds of the breath of life in the breathing remains in existence for all time. In the Easter prayer of the Act of Consecration of Man words sound from the altar, that the rejoicing of our breath has become streaming power. Easter joy speaks as new world-creating power, not only as a personal feeling of happiness. We remember how Christ after his resurrection came to his disciples, 'he breathed on them' (Jn 20:22). Is it not as though this simple tremendous picture be spoken to us so that what once occurred happen again, he 'breathed into his nostrils the breath of life' (Gn 2:7)? As though it were said to us: now the creation is again reconstituted, the divine given back to human beings? It is of the deepest meaning how in John's Gospel the breath of Christ stands together with 'peace' and 'Holy Spirit'.

For someone who experiences Christ it is still today as if Christ breathes on them. Quite spiritually but from immediate proximity the breath of life of Christ comes to them. And then there is always this double experience. A holy harmony penetrates us. A becoming fitted into the deeply hidden ordering of existence occurs. A becoming reconciled with the innermost Ground of the World. 'Peace!'

And the other: a relationship through the Holy Spirit with the whole airy regions, a life in universal spirit, which at the same time one can inhale; an encompassing from the Holy Spirit as from a new divine breath of life. The breath becomes laden with holiness. We feel that we experience exactly the same spirit that is narrated there by the disciples in parables. We gain a most inward access to the sayings of Christ in the gospels.

Albert Steffen[7] told of the passing of Rudolf Steiner that his breathing became ever quieter and more holy. The breath of someone striving to be a Christian also becomes ever holier.

At last a final secret is divined just about the breath. When breathing-in you draw all the creating world-forces into yourself. In breathing-out you give yourself back spiritually. In breathing-in you take the creating world-force into yourself, out of which Christ is born: there will be 'peace'. When breathing-out the creating world-might replies with new divine being: 'Holy Spirit' streams. In breathing-in you receive the body of Christ. In breathing-out the blood of Christ streams to you. It is not always conscious, but it can become conscious in each moment – each drawing of breath is communion.

Beauty

Why should beauty always be passed off as something heathen? Should not, somehow, the Christian element be at the same time the most beautiful, and the most beautiful at the same time Christian? Is not the highest God also the God of all beauty? That these questions were not solved in the history of Christianity shows up as a deep tragedy in the great period of the western world. Let us look to the great classic icons of our culture to solve them.

Are there sayings of Christ about beauty?

Had he said something, the austere Semitic environment with its absence of images in worship would hardly have received it. And yet tradition has washed on to the beach at least one saying. 'Yet I tell you that not even Solomon in all his splendour was not dressed like one of these' (Mt 6:29). As he spoke this, he had a flower in his hand, looked into its delicate, magnificent chalice that spoke of the Father. Beauty for him was the revelation of virtue. What a gift of foresight that this saying is preserved for us.

The artist Raphael? Has a Greek reappeared and sought the soul of Christendom? Has a Christian reappeared and grasped the language of Greece? The spirit of Greece and Christianity united – that is the first sound to be heard from a future world.

Let us compare the Aphrodite of Praxiteles with the *Sistine Madonna*. She is a goddess – unclothed. Before the reverence that the Greek felt for the human body as God's work of art, we all shrivel up as cripples. All our views about our body and the way we treat it appear to the Greeks as heathen barbarism. When the Greek lawyer stripped Phryne, the courtesan, before her judges to gain her acquittal, this was no base act; he called on the spirit of Greece itself, on their souls: *Kalokagathos,* the Beautiful and the True. Whoever is beautiful cannot be bad! From beauty, O man, draw forth virtue!

This whole world fades away when we allow our eyes to move to the Madonna. A completely different world has arisen in humanity. That the body is covered is but the sign that it is itself the covering for a being residing in it. Everything is expression. Everything is meaningful. Everything is spirit. And consequently everything is also movement. Aphrodite stands in eternal, exemplary stillness. Her hands are still concerned with her body even when in a gesture that has come to rest. The hands of the Madonna do not protect her own body; they hold the Child! Humanity has taken an enormous step into the realms of spirit. Aphrodite or Venus is pictured correctly in stone, Rudolf Steiner pronounced; the Madonna in living material, wood. Basically, a Venus in wood is just as false as a Madonna in stone.

The contrast is revealed most clearly in the eyes. Even the most beautiful Aphrodite beholds us without eyes. She looks past us into the distance. Did the Greeks know anything at all of what we experience in the human eye as the wonderful revealer of the spirit? When we listen to a Greek speaking about eyes, he speaks here too of the form: Hera with the cow's eyes. But there is still more. Through the empty eyes of Aphrodite, a world of the gods looks in on us. The soul does not yet dwell in the human being. Consequently we behold the working place of the gods through the person.

The most glorious thing in Raphael's revealing picture is the eyes of the Madonna next to the eyes of the child Jesus. The work was created with the consent of these pairs of eyes. What is a closed bud in the eyes of the Mother, bursts into the most wonderful bloom. Only such a Mother could have this Son. This Son could have only such a Mother. The heavenly shining eyes of the Child look into the world full of divining, endless beauty, free from the coyness that still holds the Mother's eyes, loosed from the shyness that still slumbers in the Mother's eyes.

Never was anything more beautiful created. Mankind matures in the Madonna like a Grail vessel waiting for the day when it receives the Christ, the light of a new world.

A world – with this we touch on a third difference. Aphrodite stands alone. But she is not alone. The whole world has condensed into this music of the body. We do not require the universe. This image falls on our soul as a ripe fruit that is gathered from the farthest widths.

Whereas Venus contains an ancient world in herself, the Madonna creates a new world from herself. The Madonna is always lovingly surrounded by a world, whether the Italians paint an open sky over her, or the Germans paint the new earth around her, a miraculous blissful *Ave* of meadows, a Paradise reappearing. The world from which she comes, the world into which she goes, is another world from the world in which we live day by day. Is it coincidence that the highest representation of the Madonna, the *Sistine Madonna* of Raphael, has around it truly the transfiguration of all worlds?

The Pope signifies of the new task of the human *body*.

St Barbara reposes full of devotion in reflection, telling of the human *soul*, or – more exactly expressed – of the etheric human being.

The Madonna herself speaks of the human *spirit*, which comes from starry heights, wants to live in heavenly realms; what is 'astral', starry, in man is called to bear the Christ.

As the divine Child, however, looks with lordly gaze into the world, free through love, carrying down heaven in his eyes, thus will live the new 'I', or *ego*, which Christ gives us, tender yet and young, but rich with all the wonders of the future. Higher and yet higher realms open behind him in pure light.

But the *earth* also wants to change. What should become of it? This is indicated by the two cherubs who peep out where the feet of the Madonna will touch the earth.

The Greeks listen to the body, how it reveals spirit. Christians listen to the spirit, how it becomes body.

Let us now compare the Greek temple with the Gothic cathedral. Greek temples are beheld from outside. They did not depend upon people being in them. They could not hold crowds of people. But in their fine delineations they was like an extension of the gods themselves. They stood there, shining white, having listened in to cosmic rhythms, born out of sacred conceptions of space – and the god lived among people. This was the expression, not the condition, that the image of the god lives in them.

The Gothic cathedral is completely different. It is built from the inside. The person at prayer creates a house around himself, 'an image after his likeness.' Gothic cathedrals are not condensed as the Greek temples from the invisible into the visible, but takes earth and stone and with it strives upwards to heaven. The Gothic cathedral speaks 'Behold the man', man who is enlivened by Christ, who strives with all strength towards heaven countering terrestrial laws.

Today true beauty is born from within, from this inner realm stirred by Christ, whether consciously apprehended or not. As the earlier beauty looks back to Paradise, so the new looks forward to the New Jerusalem. *Beauty will become apocalyptic.* Man no longer perceives beauty only in the outer world that he still sees as spirit-bearing, but he perceives the new beauty out of the inner world in which a world of becoming begins to stir.

Is it known that there really are heathen houses and Christian houses? Have you ever observed with such sentiments the villas outside large cities? Are your feelings sufficiently alive to appreciate that Christ cannot be truly worshipped in an oriental dragon house nor in a Buddhist temple, nor yet in a Greek temple, be it otherwise ever so splendid?

Christ, if he is really in the soul, educates to a new inner *sight*. Christian artists of the future will receive ever more consciously from Christ the vocation to create a new world out of inner sight. They will not imitate nature, but create beyond nature. They will create around us a thousand divinings of a higher world wanting to be born. Christ himself will accomplish this in them. The artists working from Christ will be co-creators of a new creation.

Christ in the soul is not only a new *eye,* but also a new *ear.* Devotional music, music for worship is rare today. Church music does, however, exist. Maybe a child like Bruckner had to come to give our age an inkling of this.

Christ is like a great resounding in the soul. If Plato experienced philosophy as 'a kind of sublime music', this applies in the highest sense to the Christ-experience. Christ is like a single sound in which infinite melodies dwell, from which tremendous symphonies stream down to the earth. One can understand when anthroposophy says that one day, centuries hence, the most sublime truths about Christ will be spoken through music.[8] Music will reach its highest point in the proclamation of Christ. Heavenly sounds will seek mankind 'in the dust' and bring consecration and the divine spirit.

Also *life* itself will then become an art which has its own beauty. May one not speak of the 'beauty' of St Elizabeth's life and the 'beauty' of St Francis' life? This is a beauty that does not seek to avoid the cross, but blossoms out of the cross itself.

When one returns from deep prayer or serious inner contemplation, re-entering the sensory world can be a great celebration. For this is the world in which one may now be the representative of all divine worlds.

Each word, each deed, each being should carry a message that one saw from the invisible to the visible world. A piece of heaven that one was allowed to bring down speaks out in earthly language. Life will be 'beautiful' in a divine sense in those moments when in sense-perceptible existence the 'divine glory' is manifest. The Indians shied away from maya. They could experience the sensory world only as the great illusion.

Christianity, in the greatest contrast in world-history, placed opposite the word *maya,* the word *doxa* (glory).

Certainly the sensory world, as it is, is not man's home, according to Christianity, but it should become the glory of God. 'I have given them the glory that you gave me' (Jn 17:22).

Late Summer

Space and time

There are two words in the ancient language of the Persian religion that are especially meaningful, two words that in the Indian Sanskrit no longer appear, but which still retain their ancient linguistic character in German, the word *Stern* (star) and the word *Jahr* (year). The older Avesta ends with a hymn on these two basic mysteries, releasing humanity with a view up to the infinite, to the spaces of heaven existing in themselves, and to the unending eternity, resting in itself.

How did people feel in a world in which space and time did not pass as 'forms of perception', in which the human spirit is magically confined, but which were dwellings created by the gods, temples of prayer great as the world. How pure and exalted was the worship of God in such a cosmic temple. What human nobility did this reverence lend humanity as opposed to the heathen agnosticism of the present day.

It may appear strange to people of today that a science exists, a spiritual science that also disseminates a new light of knowledge over space and time. Let someone today first take hold of the possibility in thought that space is not unending, that in not far distant heights above the earth our laws of space cease, that the fixed stars shine down from worlds in which our mathematics has nothing more to say, that the motion of the stars, the distances of the stars, the material of the stars, about which our experts speak, are the effects in the range of our senses of realities that are themselves no longer sense-perceptible. Stated differently, if we would journey out to Sirius, we would not find there an enormous globe of gas, but we would have to change ourselves to be able to be there, we would have to become spirits and find there an exalted world of spirits, whose being and deeds come to us only as an outer appearance as light and as law.

And again with time. It is valid for our solar system. Once upon a time it began here, several millions of years ago, coming from other modes of existence. One day it too will come to an end and other forms of existence will follow.

We would not fully feel the solemnity of such questions about the world if we imagined we could quickly appropriate such conceptions. But when entertained only as a possibility they work strongly on us. If we make the experiment on ourselves, how we can grasp our body with our will, then we have an inner connection to such a conception, we have an image of how the divine will bears space in itself. And everyone who goes from the day into the night and the world of dreams has the possibility to divine other forms of life in the fullness of existence than our hour-to-hour experience. Indeed, the more we lift ourselves up to the spirit, the more we learn to look up to space and time as our earthly mode of existence, and not the only one in which we can live.

It is wonderful to see how in such conceptions Zarathustra and Kant unite in a higher third. It is a human form of life indeed when we live in space-time conceptions, but still more real, less unearthly, less ghost-like, than it appears with Kant. It is to divine creative realities to which we look up in space and time, but still more transitory, with more human limitations than Zarathustra was able to express. Whoever seeks to live in this conception will soon notice that it allows him to live much better than with the Kantian, which appears desolate in comparison, but also better than with the anti-Kantian materialistic conception taking space and time naively as axiomatic, which appears dead in comparison. Is it not a grandiose, deeply religious conception of the world which can well understand space and time as realities, but as transitory? 'My times are in your hands' (Ps 31:15). 'Northern and southern lands rest in peace in his hands.'[1]

In the Act of Consecration of Man space and time arch like a temple above us. How they are present in the celebration is but one of the many details that can be found there. But how meaningfully do space and time receive their consecration here – and consequently the human being within space and time.

Where the gaze is first raised to the Father of all life, to the highest spirit of all worlds, there he appears 'weaving in the widths of space and the depths of time'. One can feel how these words have more life and immediacy for contemporary people than the words 'omnipresent' and 'eternal'. We feel that the priest who speaks these words draws a mighty world-cross over the heavens under which we live: the world-soul in the form of a cross stretched over the body of the world. This conception stems from the depths of the mysteries.[2] It is the basic fact from which we all draw life. That is what the cross on Golgotha reveals. In like manner the heavens arch above us, the heavens under which our offering, too, is worthily fulfilled.

Let us once more look up to space and time in the Act of Consecration of Man. The Spirit that weaves in the widths of space and the depths of time is called upon by us that he may hallow our offering with his holy being. It is as if on the world-cross an exalted countenance appears looking with loving-kindness upon us and receives us into the holiness of his own life. The fragrance of the greatest sacrifice in the world, the sacrifice of the Father, is wafted down like a breath of sacrificial splendour and surrounds the small sacrifice that is offered there on the altar.

Let us for a third time look upwards to space and time. At the moment after the Transubstantiation, where we make the vow to the world-Father that we wish with him to overcome sin, there is once more revealed how he, 'through Christ fulfils the revelation, the ordering of space, the course of time'. On the cross itself resurrection comes about. It starts with Christ. Christ pours out his being and life into space and time. The world-temple of space and time experiences the divine service that it has awaited. Space and time resound with divine melodies. Space and time are 'fulfilled'.

Is it coincidence that this threefold mention of space and time is at the same time a baptism? In space and time there appears first the Father of the world, then the Holy Spirit, then the divine Son. All three 'fulfil' space and time with their being and life. It is not necessary that everyone taking part should be fully conscious of what we say. Whoever lives with what takes place, space and time are baptised for them – and they in space and time.

This is preparation for the receiving of Christ in body and blood. And the receiving of Christ in body and blood is the completion of the consecration of space and time. The body of Christ is the miracle of space, the blood of Christ is the miracle of time.

As the thought of *space* – put into human words – arose in the heavenly Father, it was the sounding of cosmic music – the same cosmic music that in the fullness of time 'became flesh' in Christ. This is not pious talk; it is the experience of whoever receives the body of Christ consciously. Within him a ray of the original divine thought lights up again. A memory of this cosmic music sounds inside him. He experiences the 'body of Christ' wholly spiritually, but in complete reality.

The blood of Christ, however, lives on earth as the earthly reality of that which was in the world-Father, when the sacred flow of *time* arose in him as creating thought. Those to whom time's rhythm of life becomes really holy, experience something of the pulse-beat of Christ's blood. And the receiving, the conscious receiving of Christ's blood is like the taking up of a devoted, outpouring being who aims to be the fulfilment of all time.

We look back into the past. There stood Zarathustra, full of devotion, revealing the divine spirit who fills space and time in all the widths and distances. What a pathway leading to Christ, in whom the mystery of space and time appeared in a human life on the earth! And from there into the individual in whom working *from within,* through Christ, through his body and blood in the Lord's Supper, *space and time* now become newly consecrated. Indeed, Kant also receives his full due; space and time are forms of perception of the human mind, in which it beholds the divine. But it seeks the 'thing in itself' not behind them, but receives in them the 'Christ for us'. Christ entered into space and time, and through his consecrating sacrifice he once more turned man's abode into a temple. And he who has Christ within himself possesses heaven in every atom and eternity in every moment.

That is the *homecoming* of *space and time.*

Night and day

The light of day is extinguished. The peace of night wraps me in her healing arms. Rest, silence and darkness are like a temple that receives me. Holy sleep draws near. It is as though my soul were advancing to meet a priest who would give me his blessing. A conflict has still to be fought out with the companions of the day – thoughts that want to pursue me into the sacred precincts. Little by little the world's noise dies away. The ground of the soul grows calm and holy stars send down their rays of light to be mirrored within it. The world of the stars, wonderfully solemn and still, is patiently awaiting me. The bed on which I lie, the house in which I rest protected, disappear for my spirit. My spirit is alone with the stars. Everything that is around me here will soon pass away and be no more. But the stars carry eternity within them. Above, beneath, around me on all sides are worlds of stars, nothing but worlds of stars. I tear myself loose from the past and have nothing but stars about me. I fare over the starry sea in the boat of destiny. How well it is for me if I cannot at once fall asleep. For then I can contemplate the stars, and hear them sing their song in the distant holy heights. What will I be allowed one day to learn from all these worlds? The mysteries they bear within themselves are inexhaustible. One thing is certain – the purer I become, the more will they be able to tell me, the more will they be able to give. I can feel already their purity, for their hand is upon me to create and to fashion me, to the end that they may at length reveal themselves to me, even as a hidden sun forms and shapes the eye that shall one day behold it.

The visible world sinks down into the depths. Everything around me grows increasingly spiritual. Slowly I am lifted up into the land of the spirit. It is as though I had something to give back to the stars. The more I let myself go, the more does it rise up within me, as if that which has been bestowed upon me from the starry heights would fare homeward for one single night. With deep solemnity it takes its upward path. All at once I find myself there, giving back life to the stars, dispersing it over all the starry spaces. Yes, it is true, I come from above. Thence was I woven into a human being with an 'I'. But now the centre where I am is no longer confined. I move, hovering throughout the silent circling of the stars. Worlds of unending peace and purity breathe within me. Yet all the while I can feel how a quiet, strong, divine activity is at work. Somewhere a divine throne is set. It must surely be in the centre of all the worlds. Everything revolves around it in chaste and deepest holiness. Every star is a thought of the All-Highest, radiant, unfathomable. Every star is a pure breath of life from the all-pervading Might. I find 'I' in every star.

But what is this? The stars are no more outside me. Do they work creatively in me like my organs? I may still ask; but I cannot answer. Truth itself answers. Is there a star-body? Do the stars form a holy organism? Is my organism a star-world? It 'creates, heals and ensouls.' It is Christ. A Word with power to become a Word that lives in the stars. An innermost breath of life that fashions and creates from out of the stars. Do I carry the stars within me? Oh, that I might extinguish none. Through my body which is no longer what it was by day, I gaze into all the starry worlds. I look down from 'heaven' upon my body. But Christ holds me. He is this all. He bears me ever higher, to where I have no more power to see. I fall asleep. O wonderful rest! Received with my whole being by the pure spirit of the heavens, Christ.

Was it not now as if I had heard a summons? I seem to catch an echo of it in my being. From among a community of higher spirits one has spoken, 'He has been long enough with us; let us send him down again to the earth.'

Not that I am yet awake. But awakening is near. In the holy building wherein I have rested a super-earthly singing begins to sound. It is as though life were being poured in from the starry heights. It runs through all my veins. I seem to hear resounding from choirs above: 'Holy, holy, holy is the LORD Almighty; the whole earth is full of his glory' (Is 6:3). It is not blood that runs in my veins but the life of the stars, their song of praise. A delicate star-essence fills and purifies my body. Was Christ like this? How remote then, how utterly impossible every lower thought was for him. How godlike the flow of feeling was in him!

The light of the stars grows dimmer and changes in me to life. 'And that life was the light of all mankind' (Jn 1:4). The stars are extinguished in me and run in my veins as blood.

And now day knocks at the portal of my eye. A ray of light penetrates my eyelids, greeting me, 'Here I am again in fullness of life and I wait for you. I wait for your day.' Like an outpoured song of joy the light flows in. 'Have you not known me? Have you not been with me in the night and beheld my secret; found where I am from, and that you yourself are born of light, are inwardly related to light?'

It is as though all the stars were returning within me again in the bountiful light of the sun. As though they were waiting and watching for what is coming to birth within me. A draught of sunlight is nothing else than a draught of star-life. The night has made manifest what the day is. From the light of the sun a stream of purest blood runs over into my veins. Was it so with Christ? Was his blood pure as gentlest, holiest light? In the light of the sun does he give me to drink of his blood? Even as in the far distant ways of the stars he gives me to eat of his body? Each breath man draws of light-filled air, is it for him who knows, for him who is prepared in soul, a draught of Christ's blood?

Can I still breathe in such holiness? It must indeed come to pass – the light shall in me become life; none other than the pure light and life of Christ shall beat in my veins.

Holy awakening after holy sleep! Resurrection in the light after death in the stars.

O holy sleep and holy awakening! Come to us! Lift up our darkened life of earth to the heights that we may inwardly receive the Christ in body and in blood.

The Holy Trinity

In asking myself how it is I have come to believe in the Holy Trinity again, I can give no proof, only indications and suggestions. Dogmas of the Church have no longer power to compel us; no longer are we held in subjection by the letter of the Bible. But it is as though we heard in the depths an inner music that brings to our remembrance harmonies we listened to long ago in the sublime temple of the world, before we were sent on our earthward journey.

Even as we can trace an intuition of a threefold divine being in the teaching of the early Indians and Egyptians, so in the word of nature every plant in its threefold manifestation of root, stem and blossom sings the same holy song. And human beings themselves bear in the triune life of thinking, the feelings and the will, the indelible stamp of the Trinity who made the world. We have heard in fairytales, like Sleeping Beauty, how fairy messengers of the gods bring their gifts to the cradle of the new-born babe; but what takes place in very deed at the birth of every single child is of a majesty and wonder far surpassing these old-world stories. The divine Father of all bestows upon the newborn child a portion of his own life; He gives him the gift of *existence,* whereon life now begins its play, the life of a single individual human being. And when we have learned to behold the divine Son with the eyes of John as the eternal creative Word, he too is there spoken by the Father and breathing *life* into all existence. Likewise the Holy Spirit who gives to the new child a portion of himself. He bestows the light of *spirit,* that is woven into the awakening life like a call from its home in the light, a call that children will hear in their conscience in years to come, and will hear, too, in every truth they apprehend. *Existence, life, spirit.* The sight of the everlasting hills is not so sublime as that which human beings behold when they see in their own being the Trinity of Father, Son and Holy Spirit. Then baptism indeed becomes the great mystery of the beginning of life – for it brings to consciousness the ultimate truth of all existence. With a tongue that is hallowed anew by Christ, this truth speaks the names of those who here reveal themselves, the Father, Son and Spirit. Thus the birth is deepened through baptising.

For those with knowledge, each new day of life is a new baptism. They awake and look with joyful gratitude upon the powers that have so faithfully sustained them through the dark unconscious night. They recognise the Father, give him thanks and baptise themselves into him anew. And now they feel how their body is bathed in the divine, and new forces of life are awakening within it. They recognise the Son, thank him for his gift of life and are baptised into him anew. They look around. For what end is my fresh-born power of life? Whither shall it bear me? And behold the Spirit is there, earnestly beholding them and showing the path to the divine glory; and they recognise the Holy Spirit, who has come even into their own life; he is greeted and they are baptised into him anew.

And if such is our beginning every day, then our Sunday consecration is such to an enhanced degree. When we speak the words,

> The Father-God be in us
> The Son-God create in us
> The Spirit-God enlighten us

it is no paralysing doctrine that we utter. Rather we place ourselves joyfully into the life of the universe, into the ultimate spirit – the reality of existence – as our Christ-enlightened eyes now learn to behold it. We might wish to, and even could, speak these words as a seraph, who feels through and through that he is a spirit of light, and at the same time beholds himself in the glorious life of the world's sun, gazing with joy upon the divine gift of life that proceeds from Father, Son and Spirit – the gift out of which he himself exists. Every time we speak the words we may come nearer to the feeling of this seraph. Consequently, we speak them repeatedly, up to the measureless heights. And the cross which the priest at the altar makes as representative of humanity before the divine world – the cross with the circle of the sun – speaks to the visible world to which we belong how we strive to stand within it. It speaks into the sensory realm to which we human beings are striving as children of the heights and as messengers of the world's mysteries to all the kingdoms of creation.

'The Father-God be in us.' We bring our hand from above downwards in the direction of the ground upon which all our existence rests.

'The Son-God create in us.' We point to the far spaces where the Son brings blessing through our activities.

'The Spirit-God enlighten us.' We acknowledge the new sun that rises upon the cross and that is to become the light of our life.

With all this we are not torn away out of the earth's events; rather we are made strong for our sojourn here on earth, to do deeds mightier than before.

Of deepest significance is the little scene Goethe describes at the beginning of his autobiography *Poetry and Truth.* The boy awakes one morning with an impulse to worship God after his own fashion, free of all that is learned at school, free of all religious doctrine. A new altar is conceived and fashioned by him. He takes stones from his father's collection of minerals and places them together to form a pyramid. On the top he sets candles ready for the hour of sacrifice. Feeling strongly that he may not himself light the flame of sacrifice, he stands there with his burning-glass waiting for the sun to shine and enkindle it. A solemn awe fills him as he performs the service of worship.

Who suggested to the boy this ritual deed so full of deep meaning? We seem to hear the Time Spirit speaking with the soul of the youth. Not only is the child feeling after what the man Goethe strove his whole life to attain; in the will of the child the very striving of his age becomes manifest.

For tens and hundreds of years people have piled up a knowledge of nature. It stands there like a great mountain, but it is dead. Those who work to build it do not themselves know its end and destiny. A new altar shall arise. Upon the mountain top the flames will one day be kindled. Then it will be seen that all the work of research and enquiry that has gone on through the centuries has only served to raise higher the altar upon which the fire of the worship of God is to be rekindled. But humanity dare not themselves light the flame. Christ must come – he will come. From on high the altar will receive the fire. Like a promise that could find its way to human beings through a young and pure spirit – so seems the worship of the young Goethe. The liturgy of the future stands before us, and more, the future as liturgy. In this service of worship we catch a new song of the Holy Trinity. Before us rises the mountain built of the gifts of the earth; the living Father of all dwells within it. On the summit glows the fire wherein the Holy Spirit is manifest. From the sun comes the awakening ray, wherein God the Son gives himself to humanity. The deeper experience of nature will of itself lead human beings to where they may hearken from afar the 'Holy, holy, holy' Isaiah heard.

When the boy-priest was grown to be a man and had entered fully into life, in the *Fairy Tale* he gave expression to the innermost seeking of his soul in the picture of the subterranean temple where three kings wait to give their gifts to humanity. When the hour arrives and the old man with the lamp leads in a youth then the three kings begin to speak:

'Acknowledge the highest!' says the Golden King.
'Feed the sheep!' says the Silver King.
'The sword in the left hand the right hand free!' are
the words of the Bronze King.

We have here a picture of human longing for a new consecration of our whole being in thinking, the feelings and the will. What Goethe aspired to find is brought to us in the Act of Consecration of Man. The priest standing before the altar pictures our consecrated soul.

The *alb,* the white vestment covering him, expresses purity of thought.

The *stole* over the chest dedicates him to the love that died on Golgotha.

The *chasuble,* revealing in its changing colours the moving course of the year, and proclaiming in its forms the forces that weave the worlds, takes up his will into that which is more than the self.

The priest proclaims the Holy Trinity, without speaking a single word, as well as with every word he does speak. In the very putting on of the vestments – the sign and image of consecration – he clothes himself with the Holy Trinity; and upon the heights of the liturgy it is granted him to utter the thrice holy and solemn Song of Creation that descends from the heights of the cosmos upon our lowly earth.

And in truth all the work of the human spirit is called to perform a great and sublime baptism of the world. All knowledge and science when it is followed to the end reveals the Holy Spirit, names his name across the world. All action and creation, not alone that of the artist, if it is pure, gives birth to the divine Son. It wills to be done by the 'Christ in me'; it wills to name his name. And all being, that is deep and genuine, expresses the divine Father who goes in us through all existence.

Baptism places above the newborn child the highest hope of world-evolution; it rises up over the child like a temple, and in the temple is heard sung that ancient and holiest of songs that tells of the Triune creation of the worlds.

Wherever a human soul receives into itself some echo of this song, there the world begins to grow to its fulfilment.

Michaelmas

Autumn

We are often asked, 'I do not understand how you can speak with such assurance of the Archangel Michael. Is it possible to have a sure and certain experience of the Archangel Michael?'

The only answer one can give is to try first to enter really and truly into this season of the year and learn what it means. Many an experience can come with intensity in the autumn. People are robbed of the divine guidance that rightly belongs to their life, if they mindlessly seek refuge in the warmth within doors instead of opening their soul to the influence of autumn.

And if we go out into nature, it is all we can do to escape the overwhelming sadness that creeps about us on every hand as if to make an end of us. We look at the prickly stubble in the field, and it is as though it pierced us to the heart. We look at the falling leaves, and something within us is struck with sudden fear. We see the carpets of flowers disappear from meadow and garden, and we feel pain in those deep regions of the soul that are almost unknown even to ourselves. We see the darkness little by little steal away the sunlight, and a feeling of anxiety weighs upon our heart. One tends indeed to a deep melancholy if one enters, wide-awake in mind and soul, into the time of autumn.

We may further intensify the experience by calling to mind the way in which mankind is always affected by the contemplation of the past. The human soul is shaken to the depths when it is brought face to face with the past. Buddha gazed into the picture of a transient and dying world, and his spirit rose up in opposition That is not the world in which human beings can live. Moses sought refuge from the horror of death in the prayer: 'Lord, teach us to number our days, that we may gain a heart of wisdom' (Ps 90:12). Teutonic mythology looked into the dark twilight of a sublime death of the gods, and was filled with pain – albeit a pain lit by a far-off ray of hope.

Whoever strives to become a human being must first seek to become mankind. To face in union with all mankind the all-pervasive transience revealed in life, is to feel what it is to be a human being.

But then we can pass on from human experience to the experience of Michael. What we feel rising within us in the very face of the thousand facets of transience is a death-defying power – that is Michael. Or rather we should say more humbly, this is the power through which we can begin to sense Michael. O world of death and destruction, do what you want with me. You will never come near my real being! You will never kill my true 'I'! Feeling within us such words, we hear the voice of Michael speaking. One higher than ourselves supports us and speaks within us.

But Michael can never raise his voice in this way in anyone who has not first been touched by Christ. Easter must come to pass before Michaelmas can arise. Resurrection must have breathed its breath upon us before triumph can be awakened. Michael is part of Christ – he is not the whole Christ; he is the power and might of his sword. Autumn is the time above all when Christ fights against death, through Michael. And the battlefield is the human heart.

A new power begins to stir within us. We can sing to the waning light while we sense a growing inner sun. We can sing to the falling leaves: 'The body that is sown is perishable, it is raised imperishable' (1Cor 15:42). We can sing to the dragon of destruction that seeks to kill us with its glance, defying it. We feel the surge within us of a new pulse and a new breath. It is Michael living and creating within us. Loud and strong the song of victory swells in our heart.

This is the *Christian* experience of autumn. We greet Michael. He calls forth from the human heart that power which, working in freedom, can bring to earth the victory of heaven.

The knight

About the same time as Raphael created his exquisite picture of the Madonna who shines above time, Albrecht Dürer gave an image to the world: the Christian knight. Two ages meet; two forms of Christianity greet each other.

At that time, the inception of the modern age, it was as if Michael wanted to descend to earth and found a Michaelic Christianity. So, whoever wants to feel Michael's influence should direct their gaze especially to this turning point of time. That it was not only a single ray from Michael that alighted on to Dürer's soul is shown to us in Luther's famous hymn, *Ein' feste Burg ist unser Gott* – 'A mighty fortress is our God'. This hero's song is Dürer's 'Christian Knight' in music, the same revelation right into all the details. The mighty fortress towers into the heights in the picture: and the knight will reach it, he knows that. He carries 'a trusty shield and weapon'. But he has to journey through death and the devil, 'And were this world all devils o'er'. 'The prince of hell' – there is the devil. 'And though they take our life, goods, honour, children, wife' –

there is death. The concise words of Luther's hymn crash down like sword strokes and booming of shields. The devil's 'power' – death holds before him the inexorable hour-glass as a sign of his power – and 'craft' or cunning – the devil's louring glance has power to ensnare. But if they threaten 'watching to devour us' it does not terrify him. He knows 'all the ill that hath us now o'ertaken.' He knows he has to ride in the dark valley, but he also knows that Christ 'fights for us', will hold the field, 'shall conquer in the battle'. 'We lay it not to heart so sore; they cannot overpower us.' We can imagine the knight carries in his defiant, closed mouth the mere word that 'shall quickly slay him'. In his heart, however, he bears 'the proper Man whom God himself hath bidden.'

One wondered sometimes why in Luther's Reformation song the doctrine of justification by faith, the 'jewel of the Reformation', is not mentioned. It is there, however, intrinsically, not as a doctrine. A Christianity of the future is felt that moves above it all, a militant Christianity of deeds against the might of the adversaries. Had Michael not sent a beam of light on Luther then, he would not have succeeded. The Germans really did have a vision when Luther came to Worms, that the Archangel Michael came down to fight for them against Rome. It was the sound of a single bell before the full peal.

When we look at Dürer next to Luther we recognise the spirit of the dawning age. When we look at Dürer next to Raphael, the new distinguishes itself from that of yesterday – the Madonna approaches floating on clouds. The knight rides on the firm ground. Angels await where the foot of the Madonna will touch the threshold of the earth. Disgusting serpents cover the ground over which the knight rides. Only the faithful hound reminds one that there are also friends in the lower kingdoms. The Madonna wears a billowing veil, the knight rough armour. While the Madonna is greeted from left and right by devotion and worship, the Knight is threatened by the forces of destruction, death and the devil. The heavenly light that surrounds the Madonna and out of which the angels gaze is not to be seen with the knight. He rides into the threatening darkness of the gorge. Iron resolve is to be read on his features. A completely different world from the gracious purity on the countenance of the Mother of God, but he sees the castle rising aloft in the distance. He does not see it but he knows. He rides towards it, invincible. He masters his horse, the mystery-image of spiritual self-discipline itself. On the heights of the castle, which reaches into the sky, the cross shines over the land. The knight has the deepest connection with this cross. Self-denial.

The Madonna comes from above. That is the spirit of a Christianity which surrounded mankind with blessings a thousandfold from a higher world. Paradise. The knight strives upwards – that is the spirit of a Christianity that carries within it the force of God's seal and carries out the struggle on the earth until the castle of the future is won – the heavenly Jerusalem.

When we live into these pictures an immense amount can flow from them. When we notice what stirs in us, then Michaelic Christianity will become real in us. Its recognisable signs are spiritual strength against earthly power, Christ's will against the powers of darkness, God's fight against all devils.

Spiritual battle

We often hear people speak in a rather sentimental manner of 'conflicts of the soul'. But where are the people who of their own free will make their inner being into a field of battle? – those who know that the conflict between God and the devil has to be fought out in their own soul? – who consciously sustain within themselves this super-earthly warfare? If it is true that to be a human being means to be a fighter, then to be a Christian means to be a fighter even more so. When a person acknowledges Christ in this sense, not with his head only but with his whole being, then he is ready to enter the Order of Michael and will one day behold his leader face to face.

Life is like walking along a narrow ledge of rock, against which the waves are beating on the right hand and on the left, as if they would hurl down the human being. We go through life as in a dream. But Christ said, 'Watch.' We lose ourselves – now in this and now in that. But Christ said, 'Pray' (Mk 14:38). We do not realise that death is peering out upon us on every side. Death does not wait until the last moment of earthly life to meet us. He stands there grinning at us, every time we indulge in empty talk. He lays hands upon us every time we let ease and comfort be our master. He it is who tempts us to dream away our life, and this is true not only when we seek to 'kill time', but whenever we go about our work mechanically, whenever we simply do as others do. But most of all death has us in his grip when we talk about 'life', saying how we must get to know it and how little chance it gives us to come to ourselves. Oh, death must laugh when he hears people talk of life!

To see death, that is the first thing we learn to do in the Order of Michael. Every moment that is not filled with divine life belongs to death. Every beat of the pulse that is not made spirit by the Spirit of Christ lives in the shadow world of death. Whoever discovers that they go about on earth in the kingdom of death, that death is ever watching with a thousand eyes, show themselves to be a follower of Michael.

Nor is it death alone; the devil, too, lives on earth in countless forms. He breathes in us whenever we are filled with the glow of self-satisfaction. Every time we speak a thoughtless word, failing to let others live within us, we send forth the devil into the world. Every time some pleasure deceives us away from our task in life, the devil is trying to capture us. He surrounds us with temptations in the very place where we least expect it. Never is he nearer than when we are near to God. He waits before God's door; he crouches in ambush by the exit from the temple. He is forever finding some new corner in our soul where he may hide, and when we discover him he scornfully laughs at us. To know that we are surrounded by mighty powers of temptation, which will do their utmost to drag us into the abyss, to be alive moment by moment to the arts and wiles of the enemy, is to be awake in Michael. Every impulse that moves our life unless it is an impulse of will from the will of Christ, we share with the devil.

'Watch!' says Christ, and gives us the weapon to wield against death. His great apostle Paul knew that 'our struggle is not against flesh and blood' (Eph 6.12), but that we are the battlefield of God, where he fights with the powers of darkness. In a kind of Michael vision – perhaps with the Roman legions before his eyes – Paul beheld Christ armed with the 'helmet of salvation', the 'breast-plate of righteousness', the 'shield of faith', the 'sword of the spirit' (Eph 6:16f).

And when in our day Christ comes again to human beings, he has allowed his form to be shown as going forth upon the way into the future between death and the devil. We have often spoken of the Christ-statue in the Goetheanum, as a picture of the Christianity that is to be. Christ holds out his right hand, and because of the spirit-power that works within it, Death sinks down into the earth. Christ raises his left hand on high, and so strong is the power of the virtue within it that the great Tempter himself falls headlong to the depths.

Goethe felt the coming of the age of Michael. His Faust lives his life with his eye upon Mephistopheles. In Part One of *Faust,* Mephistopheles has more of the devil about him; in Part Two he is more like death. But the hour had not yet come when the great world-conflict of Michael was to be clearly seen. Too quickly at the end of Faust the Madonna appears again. Whoever feels today that a World-Spirit is trying to approach us and to wage within us the divine warfare against death and the devil, has discerned Michael!

Appendix

The experience of Christ through Rudolf Steiner

Before I got to know Rudolf Steiner, when my first acquaintance with his writings made meditation of renewed importance to me, I had chosen for my daily meditation the saying of Christ, 'I am the light of the world.' Today I see it was a good genie who gave me this advice. With this saying I found myself with Percival's naivety in a most sacred Grail temple. And now a development commenced that one could only wish for others in a similar fashion. Entering into this saying of Christ helped me to understand what Steiner says about John's Gospel, about Christ. And the insights of Steiner illumined for me what I learnt increasingly to feel through meditation. One may speak about this here because most people fail, they do not summon courage to trouble themselves simultaneously from without and from within to grasp the new. Receiving openly from without, working towards self-sufficiency from within; thus one gains a secure position for oneself and does not get bowled over from the richness of the far-reaching teachings. I did not know then that this very method was always recommended by Steiner himself, nor did I ever speak with him about this meditation.

But now this meditation became an Aladdin's lamp for me, lighting up the temple of John's Gospel from within. An 'I' that speaks its 'I AM' into the world – this is the original, unique revelation of John's Gospel. It is unfolded in the seven I-AM sayings:

> I am the bread of life
> I am the light of the world
> I am the gate
> I am the good shepherd
> I am the resurrection and the life
> I am the way and the truth and the life; I am the true vine.[1]

A magnificent 'I' stands before us in this sevenfold verbal organism; not an 'I', but *the* 'I' speaks here. We see into the pure human 'I', as it is conceived by the Universal Spirit itself, as it now wants to enter each single human 'I'. The sunlight in its struggle with darkness shines in the seven colours of the rainbow; the 'I am the I am' lights up now by entering into the earthly world in the different realms of life. Christ recognises himself in the bread, feels his own being as the real bread through which in truth man receives life.

In John's Gospel we are allowed to experience a unique self-knowledge of the divine 'I' while it lives in the earthly world. Something as splendid as this has never happened and can never happen again in the history of the earth. And as with the bread and with the vine, the 'I' of Christ recognises above all its identity with the light.

The stronger one experiences the 'I' in oneself, how in Christ it penetrates into the earthly human being, the more one wants to say with the Buddha: 'It shines, burns and radiates.' One experiences the 'I' as far as that intensity where it becomes light, spiritual light. And on the other hand in the light if one feels it strongly, ignoring the outer circumstances, if one allows the soul of light to work in oneself, one penetrates into the inwardness where an 'I' speaks from the light. Then one has reached the heights where before us lies the view embracing the whole world, where one so to speak 'observes God creating the world' – how the divine being speaks itself forth into nature as light from which everything comes forth: Let there be light! And how it inwardly shines as spirit, whose profoundest depths is a divine 'I'.

Notes

Foreword

1   In *Counselling and Spiritual Development,* pp. 252–68 (reprinted from *The Golden Blade* 1988, pp. 131–39).

Advent

1   Translated from the German. This political philosopher lived during the 4th Century BC. See Johnson, *The Mozi.*
2   A sermon to the monks, from the Itivuttaka. Translation made with reference to Woodward, *Minor Anthologies of the Pali Canon.*
3   Plato, *Symposium.* This version is made with reference to Shelley's translation.

Christmas

1   The author's interest in the traditional story of Widukind and Charlemagne, found in numerous nineteenth-century accounts, coincides with the fact that one of the two accepted last resting places of Widukind was the Stiftskirche in central Stuttgart.
2   An attempted translation from the poem 'Die Weihe der Nacht' by Christian Friedrich Hebbel.
3   In his autobiography, Friedrich Rittelmeyer relates during a period of enforced immobility recovering after a relapse ultimately caused by a fall in the mountains when he was laid up for weeks in a darkened room, he meditated during the Holy Nights: 'On each day of the Twelve Holy Nights a different saying of Christ came at that time like an angel wanting to visit me. Thus the essay "Twelve Holy Nights" came about ... in The Holy Year. Some of it nevertheless I have later added and edited. During these twelve holy days Christ

passed by. In his twelvefold abundance of life he revealed himself as a Child, Teacher, Physician, Judge, Saint, Sage, Hero, Prophet, Priest, King, Martyr, Lord of Glory. Every year around this time I think back with longing to those Holy Nights and days. It has been and remained the most beautiful Christmas time of my whole life.' *(Aus meinem Leben,* p. 399.)

4 Martin Luther, 1534.
5 Elijah challenged the prophets of Baal to light a sacrifice by fire. After they failed he had water poured on his sacrifice, and then prayed; fire fell and consumed the sacrifice (1K 18).

Epiphany

1 Traditionally the bones of the magi are believed to be in the Shrine of the Three Kings in Cologne Cathedral.
2 A phrase from *Thus spoke Zarathustra,* Ch. 47.
3 See, for instance Rv 21:23 and 22:5.
4 Echoing Rv 21:17.
5 The Acts of the Apostles contains three accounts of Paul's conversion: 9:1–21, 22:6–21, 26:12–18, and there are additional accounts in Paul's epistles, for instance: 1Cor 15:3–8, Gal 1.11–16.

Passiontide

1 The seven words from the cross:
   'I thirst' (Jn 19:28).
   'Father, forgive them for they know not what they do' (Lk 23:34).
   'My God, my God, why have you forsaken me?' (Mk 15:34; Mt 27:46).
   'It is finished' (Jn 19:30).
   'Woman, behold your son ... Behold your mother' (Jn 19:26f).
   'Today you will be with me in Paradise' (Lk 23:43)
   'Father into your hands I commend my spirit' (Lk 23:46).
2 The death of Buddha is described in the *Mahaparinibbana Sutta* of the *Pali Canon.* See Hermann Beckh, *Buddha's Passing: Buddha's Farewell to the Earth and his Nirvana* and *Buddha's Life and Teaching.* The death of Socrates is described at the end of Plato's dialogue *Phaedo.*
3 From Marcion, *Martyrium Polycarpi.* See also Lake, *Apostolic Fathers,* 312–45, and J.B. Lightfoot (tr.), *Apostolic Fathers,* II. iii, 363–401 in Stevenson, *A New Eusebius,* online: *www.earlychristianwritings.com/*

text/martyrdompolycarp-lake.html// and *www.christianhistoryinstitute.org/study/module/polycarp/*.

Easter

1 Friedrich Gottlieb Klopstock (1724–1803) German poet, best known for his epic poem *Der Messias.*
2 German folksong: *Wandle leuchtender und schöner, Ostersonne, deinen Lauf!*
3 As represented by Hartmann, *Philosophy of the Unconscious.*
4 Plato, *Phaedo,* 115b ff.

Ascension

1 Goethe, *Faust,* Prologue in Heaven, l. 249.
2 From the Creed of The Christian Community.

Pentecost

1 Nietzsche, *Twilight of the Idols,* Maxims and Arrows 8 (original quote: *Was mich nicht umbringt, macht mich stärker).*
2 Goethe, *Faust II,* V.5 Midnight (tr. van der Smissen).

St John's Tide

1 A nineteenth-century version of the story was written by Johann Grässe as 'Die Wunderblume auf dem Löbauer Berge' in *Der Sagenschatz des Königreich Sachsen.*
2 Nietzsche, *Thus Spoke Zarathustra,* III.9, The Return Home, p. 160.
3 It was thought to contain cyanide.

High Summer

1 *Rig-Veda* III.62.10. (*Tat savitur varenyam, bhargo devasya dhimahi, dhiyo yo nah prachodayat.*)
2 Eckermann, *Conversations with Goethe,* 330. *Die Sonne ist eine Offenbarung des Höchsten, und zwar die mächtigste, die uns Erdenkindern wahrzunehmen vergönnt ist. Ich anbete in ihr das Licht*

*und die zeugende Kraft Gottes, wodurch allein wir leben, weben und
sind und alle Pflanzen und Tiere mit uns.*

3 Francis of Assisi, 'Canticle of Brother Sun,' in Moorman, *Saint Francis
   of Assisi,* p. 111.

4 In the Mithras mysteries, for example, sun-hero was the sixth grade,
   father the seventh grade.

5 Verse by Angelus Silesius (1624–77), *Cherubinischer Wandersmann,*
   I, 173: *Das Brot ernährt dich nicht: / Was dich im Brote speist; / Ist
   Gottes ew'ges Wort, / Ist Leben und ist Geist.*

6 Goethe, *Faust II,* V.5 Midnight (tr. van der Smissen): 'The night
   comes on with deeper penetration, / Yet in my soul there shines a
   radiant light.'

7 The poet, painter, dramatist, essaying and novelist Albert
   Steffen (1884–1963), member of the Executive Council of the
   Anthroposophical Society at the Goetheanum, Switzerland, became
   president after Steiner's death in 1925.

8 Steiner, *True and False Paths,* lecture 11, Aug. 22, 1924. All the
   published translations of this lecture-cycle render this important
   passage inaccurately; for an accurate translation of the passage on
   music, see, Pals, *The Human Being as Music,* footnote 40.

Late Summer

1 Goethe, *West-östlicher Divan.*
2 It appears in the account of creation in Plato, *Timaeus.*

Michaelmas

1 The quoted passages are from *Church Hymnary,* No 454 (translated
   by Thomas Carlyle).

Appendix

A passage from the chapter bearing the title 'The Experience of Christ
through Rudolf Steiner' from Rittelmeyer, *Rudolf Steiner als Führer zu
neuem Christentum,* Stuttgart 1933. Pp. 137–39.

1 The seven I am sayings are in John 6:35, 48; 8:12; 10:7, 9; 10:11, 14;
   11:25; 14:6.

Bibliography

Beckh, Hermann, *Buddha's Life and Teaching,* forthcoming.

—, *Buddha's Passing: Buddha's Farewell to the Earth and his Nirvana,* forthcoming.

Bittleston, Adam, *Counselling and Spiritual Development,* Floris Books, UK 1988.

Crüger, Johann, *Praxis Pietatis Melica.*

Eckermann, Johann Peter, *Conversations with Goethe,* (tr. John Oxenford) 1906.

Goethe, Johann Wolfgang von, *The Fairytale of the Green Snake and the Beautiful Lily* (tr. Thomas Carlyle) wn.rsarchive.org/RelAuthors/ GoetheJW/GreenSnake.html.

—, *The Fairytale of the Green Snake and the Beautiful Lily* (tr. Donald Maclean, commentary by Adam McLean) Phanes Press, Grand Rapids, Mich. 1993 (Magnum Opus Hermetic Sourceworks No. 14).

—, *Faust* (tr. van der Smissen)

—, *West-östlicher Diwan.*

Grässe, Johann, *Der Sagenschatz des Königreich Sachsen,* 1874.

Hartmann, Eduard von, *Philosophy of the Unconscious,* (tr. W.C. Coupland) London 1884.

Johnson, Ian, *The Mozi: A Complete Translation,* Columbia University Press 2010.

Lake, Kirsopp (tr.), *Apostolic Fathers,* Loeb Classical Library, 1912.

Moorman, John R.H. *Saint Francis of Assisi,* London 1950.

Nietzsche, Friedrich, *Ecce Homo.*

—, *Götzen-Dämmerung.*

—, *Thus Spoke Zarathustra* (tr. Graham Parkes) Oxford University Press 2005.

Pals, Lea van de, *The Human Being as Music,* Leominster 2015.

Rau, Christoph, *Die beiden Jesusknaben und die dreifache Messiaserwartung der Essener,* Mayer, Stuttgart 2010.

Rittelmeyer, Friedrich, *Aus meinem Leben,* Urachhaus, Stuttgart, 1986.

—, *Rudolf Steiner als Führer zu neuem Christentum,* Stuttgart 1933.

Silesius, Angelus, *Cherubinischer Wandersmann.*

Steiner, Rudolf, *Approaching the Mystery of Golgotha* (CW 152) SteinerBooks, USA 2006.

—, *True and False Paths in Spiritual Investigation* (CW 243) Rudolf Steiner Press, UK 1985.

Stevenson, J. (ed.) *A New Eusebius,* SPCK, London 1963.

Woodward, F.L. (tr.) *Minor Anthologies of the Pali Canon,* Oxford University Press 1935, reprinted in Robert O. Ballou, (ed.) *Pocket World Bible,* London 1948/64, 124f.

Reincarnation
A Christian Perspective

Friedrich Rittelmeyer

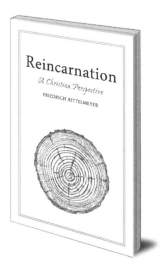

Reincarnation – by which human beings return to live on earth – is a concept most often associated with eastern philosophies rather than Christianity. In this fascinating book, Friedrich Rittelmeyer explores reincarnation from a Christian point of view, arguing that it has a place in modern Christian thought.

Rittelmeyer's approach is joyous, essentially Christian, and full of a sense of freedom as he finds a path through the pitfalls on the way to a Christ-filled acceptance of reincarnation.

Drawing on the work and inspiration of Rudolf Steiner, Rittelmeyer was able to encounter the cosmic truth of reincarnation and, wrestling with human doubt on every level, courageously grounds it in human reality.

florisbooks.co.uk

Meditation
Guidance of the Inner Life

Friedrich Rittelmeyer

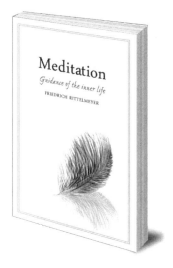

The demands of modern life are such that many people find great value in meditation. It can be hard to know where to start, however, or how to progress.

In this classic work, Friedrich Rittelmeyer recognises the difficulties we face and proposes a Christian meditative path, to guide and inspire. His work is based on the Gospel of St John and he shows how the imagery in the text can be brought alive in people's hearts through thought and imagination.

Rittelmeyer's inner training is presented with a wealth of practical advice, and a gentle trust in his reader which glows from every page.

florisbooks.co.uk

Rudolf Steiner
Enters My Life

Friedrich Rittelmeyer

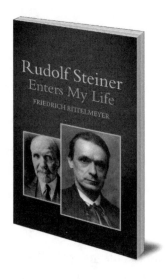

Friedrich Rittelmeyer's life took an unexpected turn when, in 1911, he encountered Rudolf Steiner for the first time. He spent the next ten years critically appraising and investigating Steiner's ideas.

This book is a fascinating and insightful autobiographical account of those years, as well a rigorous scrutiny of anthroposophy. First published in English in 1929, Rittelmeyer's honest struggle with key anthroposophical concepts has been influential for generations of people.

florisbooks.co.uk

Holy Week
A Spiritual Guide
from Palm Sunday to Easter

Emil Bock

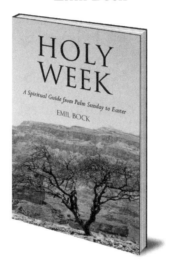

Easter Holy Week is a unique time in the Christian calendar, containing both dramatic lows and highs, as well as time for reflection and meditation.

This lovely jacketed hardback edition offers readers an inspiring guide from Palm Sunday to Easter Sunday. It vividly brings the events of Holy Week alive, enabling us to follow the mystery drama of the Passion.

It also provides opportunities for prayer and contemplation, with each day accompanied by the gospel reading which the author describes.

florisbooks.co.uk

Floris
Books

For news on all our **latest books,**
and to receive **exclusive discounts,**
join our mailing list at:

florisbooks.co.uk

Plus subscribers get a FREE book
with every online order!

We will never pass your details to anyone else.